EFFECTIVE MODERN COACHING:

PRAISE FOR EFFECTIVE MODERN COACHING

"Coaching is one of the most powerful levers any leader has to drive the performance of their team, and Myles is one of the most insightful thinkers in the field. *Effective Modern Coaching* is an inspiring work that takes a compassionate view of a very human challenge: helping individuals to reach their potential."

Richard Barkey, Founder and CEO, Imparta Ltd.

"*Effective Modern Coaching*" has been the cornerstone of executive coaching practice over the last 20 years. It is the book upon which all other coaching practices and methods have been built. The simple concept of 'performance as a function of potential minus interference' is still at the heart of what every coach does. The TGROW process has been copied and copied again in different formats, trainings and leadership programmes the world over."

Mark Hookey, Director, Performance Management, Talent Management and Learning, Swiss Re.

"A seminal work that positions coaching where it needs to be...driving performance. I have used this work in leadership programmes in many different sectors and countries and it resonates with all. The only coaching text you need."

Simon Day, Qatar Gas.

"If you buy one book on coaching this year make it this one."

Cliff Kimber, Founding Partner, BigBlueStuff.

"Myles Downey's concept is a literal realization of the coaching idea itself. His approach is fundamental, practical, modern and persistently connected with those who have attained maximum understanding of how humans learn."

Pavel Kiryukhantsev, CEO, Zest Leaders.

As a leader in fast growing markets, I find that achieving great outcomes is largely determined by how well I support the growth of helpful skills and behaviours, both with clients and with our own people. To that end

Effective Modern Coaching is the most powerful and practical toolset that I have yet found for maintaining truly effective conversations and high quality dialogue."

Jonathan Man, Executive Director, IDM Business School, South Africa and Botswana.

After 15 years as a leadership coach, *Effective Modern Coaching* is the only book I know that gets to the heart of what is uniquely powerful about coaching, and Myles is the only coach I know who writes about it with such elegance. It has been at the top of the reading list for all my clients, and this new version is even better."

Peter Nolan, Peter Nolan Associates.

"Myles Downey has a crystal clear, laser-like vision about coaching that cuts through the often messy, confusing and easy to misunderstand and misinterpret conceptions of how to define and practice this trade."

Amina Eperjesi, ACC FAB Leading Systems, Hungary.

"Myles Downey's breadth of experience as a founder business coach in the UK is very evident throughout this must-read coaching bible".

Glen McCoy, author of Guerilla Coaching.

"If the *Inner Game of Tennis* is the seminal work on coaching then *Effective Modern Coaching* is the how-to guide, an essential read for all aspiring coaches and something I return to over and over again."

James Gairdner, Director, The People Development Consultancy.

"This book is excellent - clear, very readable, pragmatic, and above all of immediate use for anyone wanting to develop their workplace coaching skills. It's a 'must have' for all coaching book shelves, whether for beginners or for experienced coaches."

Sheridan Maguire, Executive Coach.

"This book doesn't just teach you how to coach, it teaches you how to be a coach."

Dr Mike Munro Turner, aka Mike the Mentor.

"Coaching made simple, insightful and fun. This will be THE practical reference into the next decade for how leaders, managers and organizations use coaching."

John Grisby, Principle/DNA Performance and Professor of Management Practice.

Effective Modern Coaching is one of the most popular coaching books in Hungary for those who read English.

For those Hungarians who do not read English Myles came to Budapest to hold a one day workshop -with interpretation - where chapters of this new book were presented embracing Myles' knowledge and experience of his 30 years of coach work including his love for tennis and describing all the parallels he draws from sport which are very specifically linked to coaching and eloquently described in the book just as vividly as they came through in his live presentation in Budapest.

"This book gives coaches the clear, easily understandable basics to the coaching profession that is a must-read for all those who want to become well trained coaches for the benefit of their clients."

Judit Ábri von Bartheld PCC, Executive coach, Organizer of Coaching Without Borders, Hungary.

"Myles' insistence on benefits for the organization, not just for the coachee, justified investment in coaching in many organizations, which in turn fuelled rapid growth in the Executive Coaching market. His updated insights are awaited eagerly."

Mike Taylor, MD, Accelerating Experience Ltd and former Executive Director and Advisory Board member, EMCC UK.

"Genius inside. Is it a badge each of us deserves? Yes, says Myles Downey, and gives a unique blend of inspiration, knowledge and tools for revealing human potential through coaching. A fundamental book for everyone who keeps on asking questions."

Andrei Mikhailenko, Partner, Zest Leaders, Vietnam.

EFFECTIVE MODERN COACHING:

THE PRINCIPLES AND ART OF SUCCESSFUL BUSINESS COACHING

MYLES DOWNEY

MADRID | MEXICO CITY | LONDON
NEW YORK | BUENOS AIRES
BOGOTA | SHANGHAI | NEW DELHI

Published by
LID Publishing Limited
The Record Hall, Studio 204,
16-16a Baldwins Gardens,
London EC1N 7RJ, UK

info@lidpublishing.com
www.lidpublishing.com

A member of:

www.businesspublishersroundtable.com

Reprinted in 2015, 2016, 2017 (twice), 2018, 2019 (twice)

Printed in Great Britain by TJ International
ISBN: 978-1-907794-76-6

Cover & page design: Laura Hawkins

CONTENTS

Acknowledgments

Many people have contributed to my learning, and have thus contributed to this book: coaches, mentors, teachers, and professional friends and colleagues who have helped me over a period of about 30 years. And then there are all the people I have coached or trained to coach.

I would particularly like to thank Alan Fine, Graham Alexander, Martin Brooks, Sir John Whitmore, Susie Morell, Ben Cannon, Caroline Harris, Charles Sherno, Chris Morgan, Tony Morgan and Philip Goldman. Charles Brook, Judith Firman, Jane Meyler, Sheridan Maguire, Anne Scoular, Dr Mike Turner, Trevor Waldock, David Webster, Peter Nolan, and Barry Curnow. A word of thanks to Tim Gallwey for writing The Inner Game of Tennis, a book that opened up a new world for me. In recent years, two people have pushed my learning, at personal and professional levels, more than any others, sometimes to the point where it hurts: Cliff Kimber and Richard Merrick. Thank you.

Myles Downey

Introduction

Many years ago, in the heyday of my previous business, the School of Coaching, I attended the last day of a 'coaches' programme' being delivered by two colleagues. This was what we called a 'friends and charities' programme, which enabled us to provide the training to people who could not justify the full programme fees. It also provided the opportunity for my colleagues to complete their own training as programme leaders. There was one participant, the head teacher of a local school, who had not been the easiest of participants to work with. As the programme closed he said, in words close to these: 'I know that I have not been the easiest participant, but what you don't know is that, as a function of this programme, I have turned my school into a learning organization of 2,000 people—and that includes the teachers!'

This drew a laugh. I was left with a picture: I had dropped a pebble into a pool, the ripples had been picked up and passed on by my colleagues, and then picked up in turn by the participants, just one of whom had himself impacted on 2,000 people. This book has a similar intent: to send some ripples far and wide. Ripples about how to enable the inherent genius in others. Without, I hope, being pretentious, complicated, or overwrought, it is about a simple skill, which, properly practised, has a profound impact.

My first book on coaching—Effective Coaching, upon which this volume is based—was published in 1999. Much has changed since then. The generation of people active in the workplace now have a different set of values, a different outlook that's less compliant and has a greater sense of self. More difficult to 'command and control'. And organizations—the employers—are struggling to find ways to respond, not just to this generation, but also to a vastly more volatile world.

To put this in context, let me suggest that one thread in the story of the 20th century is the drive toward ever-greater efficiency, from Henry Ford's production line to total quality management and business process re-engineering through to Six Sigma and Lean management techniques. (A Six Sigma process is one in which 99.99966% of the products manufactured are expected to be free of defects—that is, 3.4 defective parts per million.)

You could say we know how to do efficiency. These approaches are powerful and appropriate when applied to manufacturing processes (inanimate objects) but not so good when applied to the animate (human beings). And unfortunately, in education systems where learning is designed to create 'units of production and consumption', and in our management and management-development systems, this is just what we have done.

Take 'competencies' (please!). Why settle for competence when genius is possible? Progress will not come from 'competence', or from greater efficiency. Today's organizations don't need more efficiency—they need human creativity and imagination. Tightening the process will not deliver these things. In fact, it disables genius.

Responding appropriately is, in part, about finding ways to engage the people in organizations and help them develop and deploy their talents—to their own benefit and to that of the organization. It is about enabling genius.

Here is the irony: coaching is increasingly of vital importance to the success of business organization and to the flourishing of individuals (these two being symbiotic). Coaching is also facing the possibility, in becoming institutionalized, of losing its subversive, provocative edge. The edge that seeks out new possibilities, new horizons—new ways of being and doing things.

Those of us who evangelize coaching and are passionate about it might remember that coaching is not a thing in and of itself—it does not have any validity outside of the outcome. The sports coach is there to deliver a better performance. Coaching is the servant of something—a process, a means of delivery. It is the means in service of an end. It's a verb, not a noun.

In the two previous editions of Effective Coaching I have been guilty of trying to 'prove' that my approach to coaching is the one and true model, and that all others were heretical. Not helpful! Coaching as a noun. This book, however, is intended to be more helpful. The effective coaching model is a proven approach. The book describes—in the most comprehensive manner I am capable of—the skills of coaching and how they might be applied. And I am clearer, and more courageous, in my pronouncements today than I was in 1999.

In the late 20th century, in a world driven by efficiency and compliance, to suggest that coaching was about individual genius, self-expression, and autonomy would have resulted in a very small client base. Today, there is a vital need to enable individual genius—while finding the means to ensure that this, in turn, results in a more powerful organization.

I fundamentally believe that the natural state of the human being is to be fully expressed, uninhibited, and without doubt or fear. To be able to perform, learn, and enjoy. A state in which there is access to all the innate resources born to us. Genius.

I believe that we are at our best in the company of others: not dependent, not independent, but interdependent. I hold that such actualization is seldom (if ever) achieved alone, but made possible in community or with the guidance of a gifted other—one who has the capacity and courage to hold a different kind of conversation, a conversation that lets one's thinking unfold, lets one's imagination, intuition, and creativity loose, and in so doing allows one to come to one's own understanding.

Such a conversation is a dangerous conversation. It demands that one step outside of one's fear and doubt—one's shoulds, musts, and have tos—and into your innate genius.

I believe that our business organizations can be the hothouses for these different and dangerous conversations: conversations that enable genius, in the best interests of employees, organizations, and stakeholders.

This book is, however, different from my first book. It offers fresh thinking and new models, providing greater clarity and a revised structure that makes it easier to read. It is both an introduction for those new to coaching, and, given its comprehensive nature, a reminder and a reference for more experience coaches. It is intended for coaches, both practising and novice. It is intended for managers and leaders—I believe that coaching is a fundamental skill for people in management positions. It is also intended for anyone who has an interest in enabling genius in others.

I was surprised to find that Effective Coaching was required reading on a leadership programme in a global consulting organization, and similarly for a number of training programmes for sports coaches, and that teachers, parents, and many others have found value in reading it. In response, I have written this book with people in these and similar positions in mind.

I hope you find Modern Effective Coaching to be of value, and to be an enjoyable read.

EFFECTIVE COACHING DEFINED

– CHAPTER 1 –

A conversation

'Henry! How are you?'

'God knows!'

'What do you mean?'

'I'm on autopilot. I've had about 17 hours sleep all week.'

Just so you, the reader, know, we are in the offices of Brand plc. by the water cooler on the fourth floor.

'Wow. How's that?'

'You don't want to know.'

'Try me.'

'How long do you have?'

'Seriously? About half an hour now, but if we need it I have an hour toward the end of the day, after 4:30.'

'Yeah, maybe we should talk. We can sit over there.'

'Fine. Let me fill my glass. So … what's happening?'
'It feels like I'm working flat-out and getting nowhere.'

There's a pause. Melanie says nothing. Henry continues.

'You know I have an objective to develop our offering for the Public Sector?'

'Of course. We worked through it before.'

'It's become more complex since then.'

'In what way?'

'In how many ways, more like. The people I'm working with are a bunch of halfwits, for a start. Nothing that I ask them to do gets done, or if it does it's so bad that I have to re-do it myself. My own team is the worst, the guys from finance are just slow, but at least they get it done.'

'What else?'

'What else? Is that not enough for you?'

'Well, you said "complex" and while...'

'No, no, there's more. We made some assumptions about the costs at the very beginning and we tested them with a number of potential clients. Of course, what we did not anticipate was that the Government would stop funding centrally and require the departments to do this from there own budgets.'

'They still want it, the departments?'

'More then ever, as far as we can tell. They've just got less money.'

'What else?'

'Wh...Sorry. Stress. The really difficult bit is that our glorious leader, Steve, is breathing down our necks – my neck mostly – asking for one thing, and Jeremy from Marketing is asking for another with no less intensity.'

'What else?'

Henry shakes his head. Nothing.

'Then, if I have understood, there are three parts to this; the ability of the project team; a shift in the financial parameters and the differing needs of our two friends, Steve and Jeremy.'

'That's right. Although, on the third point, it's as much about the pressure they put on me as it is about their 'needs', as you put it?'

'Ok. So four things then, including the pressure they are putting on you. Which would be most interesting to talk about first?'

'Sorting out the boys'

'Steve and Jeremy. You're sure?'

'Yes, I think so.'

'It's just that the feedback from your team in the last 360, if you remember, suggested that you were overly controlling and unwilling to delegate. I'm just wondering if that's part of this?

'Fair enough. I think I've been doing better on that since our last conversation—at least until this project got silly. I really think I need to sort the Steve-and-Jeremy issue first. If they let us get on with it we could sort the other things.'

'So, tell me what's going on with them?'

'You know how it is where we sit, all open-plan. Steve and Jeremy both have to walk through my area to get to their offices, so they're forever "dropping in". That would be bad enough, but they are both looking for different things. Steve wants us to cut this thing to the bare bones so that he can show the executive team how good he is at managing costs, and Jeremy wants this to be the sexiest thing ever, all bells and whistles, which he thinks will make it easier to sell, so that he can show the exec that he can bring our services to different markets. They are both leaning on me—and the others in the team—making demands that the other overturns. And since one of them is likely to be next head of division, you don't want to upset either.'

'So how are you managing?'

'I guess we're just agreeing with both of them and hoping they don't notice. Other than that, I just try and steer my way through.'
'What does that mean?'

'I make the best guess that I can, given the information, and make sure that I present it to them individually, so that I can speak up the things that support their needs and conceal the things that don't. It's bloody exhausting.'

Henry starts laughing. 'What?'

'They never do notice. They're too busy playing politics to take the time to get inside the project.'

'What can you do? What options do you have?'

'If I thought I had options …'

'Jesus, Henry, don't be so cantankerous.'

'Sorry. It's the stress. Again.'

'Tell me, in an ideal world, how would things be different?'

There's a pause while Henry thinks.

'There would be a clear set of objectives that we had all agreed. That sounds so pathetic. You know there are objectives already. But Steve and Jeremy have not bought into them, and they are now using the fact that there's a shift in the financing to bend things to their own ends.'

'So what do you need to do?'

'I need to get to a new set of objectives that account for the current situation, and that all parties agree to.'

'How might you achieve that?'

'Arrange some kind of meeting. Although first I'd have to get marketing to complete the survey, then finance would have to cost the various options …'

'What are you thinking?'

'I said earlier that I just try and steer my way through, but that's the wrong approach completely.'

'It is?'

'Of course. If I try and find a compromise I please no one. The other option, I've just realized, is to identify the various possibilities with the costings worked out, and then to get Steve, Jeremy, and the others to make a binding decision. We'd have to do it in a very pragmatic, business-like way, so that the personal agendas were minimized.'

'So what needs to happen from here?'

'The first step is to get my own team on board so that we complete the survey and the costings exercise as quickly as possible.'

'But you said they weren't performing well.'

'I know. I was a bit unfair. It's impossible to perform well when the goal posts keep moving and people change the rules. Plus, I think that the prospect of getting our two friends off our collective back will be so appealing that they'll pull out all the stops.'

'And then?'

'Then arrange a meeting at which we present the possibilities. We'd need to get Mac there as well. This could also solve the second issue—the fact that the source of funding has changed—because I'll have more people to help me work through.' (Mac is the current head of division.)

'How confident are you that this will work?'
'On a scale of one to ten, about an eight.'

'There were three—no, four—issues at the beginning, and it sounds like you've got some movement on three of them. What about the team/control matter?'

'I really do think that has shifted. And I also think that part of the problem was that we had conflicting objectives, caused by my own indecision, and by Steve and Jeremy. The 360 will happen again in about three months. Maybe we should look at it together then.'

'Fine.'

'Thanks, Melanie.'

Coaching

When I run coaching skills workshops, I nearly always start by getting someone from the group to come to the front and coach them on a real, business issue. This is the best way I know of getting people to think about coaching, aside from which it can be fairly dramatic as the coaching is real—it is not a roleplaying exercise, and there is no guarantee that it is going to work out. The conversation played out above is an example of the kind of issue that people bring to these sessions, although it is presented here in such a way that Melanie could be either Henry's manager, a colleague, an internal change agent or a professional coach from outside the organization.

At the end of the coaching demonstration, I ask the other participants a simple question: 'What did you notice?' Here are some typical responses:

'You really listened.'

'You asked a lot of questions.'

'You spent a lot of time trying to understand.'
'You summarized frequently.'

'You let him work it out for himself.'

'You added no value.'

'You did not add in anything, like suggestions or advice.'

'I had so many thoughts about what he should do.'

'What if the course of action they had decided on was wrong?'

'That was not coaching, it was more like counselling.'

'If I did that in my office, they'd think I had gone mad.'

'In my country, the manager has to know the answer or he'd lose credibility.'

'What happens if the course of action the person chooses is in opposition to the company's plans?'

'I just don't have the time to do that.'

The thing that stands out for most people is that the person being coached—the player—does most of the work. (Note that I use the word 'player' in place of the word 'coachee'. This is because I think 'coachee' is an ugly word, and because it has the suffix '-ee' at the end, which denotes someone who has something *done* unto them—think 'divorcee'. Player suggests enjoyment, and that he or she is the primary person.)

You may remember from reading comics in your youth the thought bubble over a character's head, showing what he or she is thinking. A great coach and former colleague, Heather Dawson, used to ask: 'Over whose head is the thought bubble?' This is probably the simplest way I have to communicate what effective coaching is about. Ideally, the thought bubble should be over the player's head. Not the coach's.

The player does the thinking, not the coach. The coach's job is to create an environment where the player can do their very best thinking.

People come to these workshops to learn about coaching. Their initial expectations are that it has something to do with passing on either knowledge, experience, expertise, or wisdom, or that it is in some sense an applied psychology—that there are techniques and tools that can be learnt and then implemented to make people more motivated. What they actually discover, however, is that coaching is both less and more than that: less in that the fundamentals are very simple, and more in that the impact of becoming a more effective coach is greater than might initially be expected. In this book, I will try to answer the questions raised above and to give a sense of the productivity, fulfillment and joy that can arise from effective coaching.

– CHAPTER 2 –

Coaching described

The conversation in chapter 1 is a good example of effective coaching. The questions and objections listed reflect a general confusion about what coaching is, what its function is, and how it fits in the workplace. In this chapter, I want to bring some clarity to the 'territory', and to begin to describe effective coaching. More specific definitions will follow in the next chapter—this chapter is more about bringing the core ideas to life in a descriptive manner. In doing this, I will give a brief overview of the field and seek to establish a foundation for the rest of the book. (The question about how coaching fits in the workplace is largely addressed in chapter 11.)

The territory and the confusion

'Coaching is for failures.'
'Coaching is a mark of my status (the company pays for my executive coach).'
'Coaching is an emerging profession.'
'Coaching is a management competency.'
'Coaching is a fad.'
'Coaching can save the world.'
'Coaching is a second career.' *(Soon-to-retire HR manager)*
'Coaching is … not my job.' *(Manager, coaching workshop)*

Coaching means different things to different people, depending on who they are, what they are doing, and what their experience of coaching is. A human resources manager taking early retirement and thinking about how he might use the next stage of his life productively will have a very different perspective from the manager in an IT business who has just been told to attend a workshop on coaching skills, when what she really wants to do is to continue developing software. There is no commonly held definition of coaching. In a way, this is a good thing, because definitions, while giving clarity, can also exclude other possibilities and make other notions—perhaps valuable ones—wrong.

If I tell someone that I am a coach, the immediate question is: 'In which sport?' Most people's initial exposure to coaching is through sport, and in almost all sports, coaching is built around the idea that it is essentially the transfer of knowledge. The coach is the expert—he or she knows the correct technique, and will tell you how to perform. As this knowledge/expert model is also the predominant model in education systems, it is hardly surprising then that, in the world of work, people make similar assumptions about coaching.

The disciplines of psychology and psychotherapy offer another perspective on coaching, and indeed there is a point of view that only people with qualifications in one of the above should be allowed to coach. The conclusion to that argument can only be that all of us—managers, parents, teachers, spouses, partners, siblings, colleagues and friends—should be trained therapists. Or cease talking to each other. Because coaching is, in a sense, happening all the time: any time a person discusses with another how to do something, that's coaching.

There is something about the first part of the 'conclusion' that I find appealing, and I don't deny that there are times when not talking would resolve many problems. But the reality is that neither 'solution' is practical. Silence may be golden, but it would also be very dull, and coaching is going on all around us, often with beneficial results. And the world is not full of therapists—even though it might seem like it at times.

A range of other approaches to coaching have roots in the post-Maslow self-actualization movement, such as transformational technology and appreciative enquiry, or hybrids—in this case with psychology—such as neuro-linguistic programming. If you read around the territory for a while, you will also get to pop psychology—self-help, positive thinking, and religious schools of thought. But it does not stop there. You can have executive coaching, developmental coaching, and performance coaching. Senior executives get coached because they do not have the time or inclination to go to the appropriate training programme. Those, that is, who are willing to admit that they have something to learn!

And then there is life-coaching. While I am sure that there are some life coaches out there doing good work in a responsible manner, there are also a lot of people doing the work of counsellors without anything like the appropriate training. To this list I can also add mentoring.

Coaching training itself contributes to the confusion. Training is available in coaching at almost every level, and in almost every form imaginable. At one extreme, you can get a master's degree, and at the other a distance-learning programme; a couple of years' academic study, or a couple of phone calls.

The origin of the word 'coaching' is surprisingly obvious. It comes from 'coach'—a wheeled vehicle used to carry people from one place to another. The name comes from the town in Hungary, Kocks, where these vehicles were apparently first made. The first known usage of 'coach' that comes close to the sense in which it is used in this book occurs in the middle 1800s in British universities, principally Oxford and Cambridge, where the term was given to an independent tutor who 'carried' the student through the exams. Then we find it being used in the middle of the 1900s, in reference to sports coaches at American universities. After that, coming out of the post-war humanistic resurgence, one begins to find the word being used as it is today, in what might now be called life-coaching. Interestingly, business coaching was, for the most part, developed in the UK, beginning in the early 1980s.

Given all the different sources, inspirations, and applications, it is no wonder that there is confusion. Coaching is in danger of being defined by the inputs that the philosophies, models, and approaches it champions bring with them, rather than by the outputs: the results that we need in our places of work.

The primary output, I would suggest, is that we have people in our places of work that can perform at the top end of their potential. And I am hoping—by starting with some ideas about how to access that potential—to simplify this world of coaching.

The genius in the player

I prefer the word 'genius' to the word 'potential'. 'Potential' has been bandied about so much that it has lost all meaning. It just floats by us and changes nothing.

'Genius' is different. In common usage, the word is given to those who reach extraordinary levels of performance, and who have been blessed with a gift, either by some deity or that has come down from previous generation through their genes. As I will show in chapter 15, however, the situation is not that straightforward. We know quite a lot about the process of becoming a genius, and that it is available to us all. That's what makes the word genius different. Once you are clear that genius is not the preserve of the few, it becomes an opportunity—and a challenge. Accessing that genius is a goal of effective coaching.

The following model is a profound and simple way of understanding something about how to do that, and is therefore a foundational idea in effective coaching.

The Inner Game of Tennis is one of most influential books on performance and learning of the last 40 years. Written by Timothy Gallwey in 1974, it remains in print today and has been followed by other titles, including *The Inner Game of Work.* The original book caused a huge stir when it was published, and the ideas in it—which apply to many areas of life beyond the tennis court—have been embraced by many thousands of people all over the world.

Let me introduce you to one of the core concepts, which starts with two words, as below. Gallwey used the word 'potential', and since this is his model, I will stick with that.

Potential   Performance

I have put a gap between the two words because there is always a gap between performance and potential. It is a huge gap. Even in the most ordinary activity, no matter how good someone is at it, he or she can always do better. There is something in the gap, and understanding what it is can help bridge it. I can remember occasions of becoming anxious and distracted while playing competitive tennis. The little voice inside my head would start saying things like this:

'You can't let this loser win—what would they say in the changing room?'
'Watch the ball.'
'I hope he doesn't serve to my backhand.'
'Just push it back into play. Play safe.'
'No, hit it cross-court.'
'You idiot.'

Gallwey called thoughts like these 'interference'. Interference is usually rooted in fear and doubt. I would argue that nothing gets in the way of peak performance more than doubt. So the model becomes

Potential minus interference is equal to performance

Thus one way to increase performance is to reduce the interference. As the interference is reduced, more potential is available.
Interference crops up in many forms. Here is a partial list that you might find familiar:

- Fear (of losing, of winning, of making a fool of yourself)
- Lack of self-confidence
- Trying too hard
- Trying for perfection
- Trying to impress
- Anger and frustration
- Boredom
- A busy mind.

One of the ways to reduce interference is to focus attention. When attention is focused, the player enters a mental state in which he can learn and perform at his best. Gallwey called that mental state 'relaxed concentration'. Most people that I speak to have had an experience of this mental state, also called 'flow'. For some, it is a profound and moving experience, very often coming when they are engaged in a physical activity. A friend of mine used to race motorbikes and, occasionally, when he was absolutely at the limit, with his attention glued to the rider in front of him, he would get into flow. His thoughts and actions would become one, time would seem to slow down, and the noise of the engines appear to diminish. In this state, he would sense exactly when the rider in front was going to make a mistake and be able to capitalize on it without hesitation.

Being in flow does not have to be quite so dramatic. It can occur during such mundane activities as writing. You sit down at your desk and get started. You make a number of false starts; it is just not quite right. You get up, close the door, sit down, and start again. Suddenly, the words begin to come. You become engrossed in the task. You look at your watch; an hour has gone by, and you did not even notice it. The report is half written. From the perspective of the 'inner game', a key part of the line manager or coach's role is to help reduce the interference that affects the people he works with. This would be a remarkable shift of focus.

I will try to give some more life to this core concept by describing a demonstration that a colleague gave at a coaching skills workshop. It is an adaptation of an exercise that Gallwey uses, and it shows quite clearly what happens when the coach is truly committed to the player's learning and does not get in the way of that learning with instructions, advice, or suggestions. Interestingly, this approach is not reliant on the coach being an expert in the topic of the session. In fact, there is not one instruction or suggestion in the whole session; the coach is working with the individual's capacity to learn.

My understanding is that this learning capacity is wrapped up in an individual's 'potential'. Learning is hard-wired.

The topic for this session is 'how to improve catching'—in this case, catching a ball. It requires a willing volunteer from the group who believes that he cannot catch.

The coach positioned himself about 12 feet away from the volunteer and addressed him: 'To start with, let's just see if you can catch at all. OK?' The volunteer, Peter, nodded but did not say anything. The coach threw a ball to him. Peter held out both hands stiffly in front of himself, his face screwing up with fear and anticipation. The ball passed just over the top of his hands, thumped into his chest, and fell to the floor. Embarrassed, Peter grew even more tense.

The coach threw another ball. Peter reached out, as before, and missed completely. The coach threw another with the same result.

'Is that what you would expect?' the coach asked.

'Absolutely,' Peter replied in a small voice. 'I told you I couldn't catch and never could. Teachers in school would put me in goal just to get a laugh.'

'Is that what you're thinking when I throw the ball?'

'That, and … and all these people watching.'

The coach looked around at the people, some of whom had stood up and formed a loose circle around him and Peter.

'Ah, don't worry about us' came a kindly voice.
The coach paused and caught Peter's attention again. 'Tell me, Peter,' he said, 'if your catching was to get better, how would we know?'

'Well, I'd catch them, wouldn't I?'

'All of them?'

'Some of them.'

'How many out of ten?'

'Would you throw them in exactly the same way as before?' Peter enquired suspiciously. The coach nodded. 'Then to catch one out of ten would be amazing.'

'I know. And what would give you a real sense of achievement?'

'I'll say three out of ten.'

'OK. Stay with me—I'm going to throw you some more balls. What I want you to do is watch the ball when it's in flight and, when you've caught it, tell me what you noticed about it. OK?'

'So I'm to tell you what I notice about the ball when it's flying toward me?'

'Exactly.'

The coach threw a ball. It brushed Peter's fingers as it went by him.

'What did you notice about the ball?'

'Nothing.'

'OK. Tell me what you notice about this one.'

Again he threw a ball, and again Peter failed to catch.

'It's just yellow, greeny-yellow.'

Peter's response drew a snigger from the group. Without taking his eyes from Peter, the coach put a finger across his lips and the laughter stopped.

'Fine,' he said. 'Tell me what you notice this time.' He threw another.

'It's got some writing on it,' said Peter, as the ball bounced out of the palm of his hand.

'Fine, so you notice the colour and the writing. Which is most interesting?'

'The writing.'

'OK. Tell me some more about the writing.' He threw a ball again.

'The writing is spinning, the ball is spinning,' said Peter, as he caught the ball. There was a sharp intake of breath from behind. The coach did not respond.

'Shall we stay with the spin?' he asked. Peter nodded. 'Tell me what you notice about the spin.' Once more the coach threw a ball.

'It's spinning toward me, quite fast,' said Peter, as he caught again.

'You noticed both the direction and the speed of the spin. Which is most interesting?'

Peter paused. He threw the ball back to the coach. 'Er ... the direction.'

'OK. Tell me which way this one is spinning,' the coach asked, and then threw a ball. Peter reached out toward the ball and gracefully caught it, pulling his hands back toward himself like a confident cricket player. He was completely relaxed, focused.

'The top is spinning toward me, and a little to the side.'

'Which side?'

'This way,' Peter said, describing the direction with his finger in the air.

'And this one?' the coach asked, as he threw another.

'Spinning the other way.'

'And this one?'

This one Peter completely failed to catch the ball.

'What did you notice that time?'

'Nothing at all.'

'So where was your attention?'

Peter's face creased into a big grin. 'I was thinking that I was catching for the first time in my life. Incredible!' He started laughing. The group clapped and laughed with him. 'How did you do that?'

'We'll come back to that. Tell me, how did you do in relation to our goal—to catch three out of ten?'

'I've no idea. I must have caught three, though.'

One of the other participants in the workshop observed: 'You caught five out of eight by my counting.'

'Wow. That many?'

'Peter, are you willing to stop the exercise?'

'Ah, just one more … no, go on, it's fine.'

The coach turned to the participant who had made the observation. 'What did you notice about the exercise?'

The participant thought for a second. 'Mostly that you didn't tell him how to catch. You gave him no technical instruction.'

'Anything else?' the coach asked.

Someone else added in: 'What I noticed was how you made Peter concentrate.'

'How did I do that?'

There was a pause.

'You just asked him what he noticed ...'

'Yes.'

'And then ...'

Here Peter joined in. 'I noticed the colour and the writing ... and you asked me to choose one ... and I chose the writing.'

'Yes. And then?'

Nobody seemed to remember, so the coach filled in the blank. 'I think I asked you to tell me what you noticed about the writing.'

'That's right, that's when I noticed that it was spinning,' Peter answered.

'I see what you were doing,' another participant said. 'Each time Peter looked at the ball, he noticed something more—some more detail—so after a while, he was concentrating completely.'

'Yes,' Peter added in, 'and the more I concentrated, the less I noticed the other people, and I kind of forgot that I couldn't catch.'

Another voice from the group asked: 'But how did he learn how to catch?'

'To a degree, he already knew. Peter's seen others doing it, and he's tried before. So he had some information already. But more importantly, with each attempt he learnt something more, unconsciously. Peter always had the potential to learn how to catch. Notice I did not say that there was a "great catcher" within him just waiting to get out; this is about the potential to learn quickly, and in a way that's fun. It's just that self-doubt and fear were getting in the way of the learning. When he got really focused, the fear and doubt were forgotten, and his natural ability to learn came to the fore. And I'll bet that if I had tried to teach in the more traditional way, and given instructions, he would have got more tense and fearful, and would have failed yet again.'

It is difficult to communicate on paper just how extraordinary the exercise described above is. Most people who witness it are completely taken by surprise. They have never seen such a dramatic shift in performance. They have never seen someone learn so quickly. They have seldom seen so much joy in so simple an exercise.

Having seen the exercise, most people want to know what happened, and what the coach did. The realization that the coach did very little, and that there was no technical instruction involved, is the second surprise of the day. That brings me back to an earlier idea: keeping the thought-bubble over the head of the player. In a sense, the paradigm that most people operate from—that tells them about how people learn, and how quickly they can learn—has been blown apart. The coach's responsibility, therefore, is not to teach but to facilitate learning.

Stuck and unstuck

The fundamental precept of effective coaching is that the coach is primarily reliant on the players' capacities, their potential, and their genius to enable them to progress. And then there is interference.

A great coach and friend of mine, Peter Nolan, talks about 'being stuck' and 'getting unstuck'. He had been doing some work with a group of long-term unemployed people. One of the first things he did was to visit the agency where they were being helped to find their way back into work. He noticed the helpers—the consultants—held all the cards. They sat behind their desks, read in their files, consulted their computers, and prescribed what should be done, right down to the smallest details: 'Remember to wear your suit,' 'Take the 45A bus,' 'Don't be late.' The 'clients' sat meekly and nodded, feeling patronized and disempowered. These clients were, in Peter's words, stuck, and the very people who were supposed to be helping them were actually causing them to become even more stuck.

Peter was telling me this in a pub while we had lunch, and as we ate he drew a picture on a napkin. It was of a 'stickman' clinging on to the side of a cliff for dear life, too terrified to move, fearful that even lifting a finger would precipitate a fall. The inference, of course, was that the participants in his programme were similarly stuck. Peter then drew a cartoon of the consultant as a larger-than-life angel moving in to rescue the poor individual on the cliff. This, he said, drew short laughs of recognition from the participants. The job of the consultant, as Peter observed it, was to rescue the clients from the cliff face and to put them, well, anywhere else—but they were still unable to move; still stuck.

Peter saw the job differently. He saw it as being about helping the client become unstuck and able to move for himself. We are all stuck in some way, and the job of coaching is to help us get unstuck, and get moving, for ourselves.

– CHAPTER 3 –

The effective coaching proposition

This chapter lays out my proposition for effective coaching. It is what I believe coaching can be. The next chapter is a description of the effective coaching model—the nuts and bolts. In leading up to the proposition, I will play out a number of definitions of coaching in order to continue to build a full sense of the concept.

A definition

The following is a definition of coaching that has some currency and is used at the School of Coaching:

Coaching is the art of facilitating the performance, learning, and development of another.

It is worth looking at some of the individual words in this definition. I will start with the word **performance**. Coaching in business is ultimately concerned with performance, and anything a coach might say or do should be driven by the intention to improve it. Improved performance may relate to the execution of a specific task or project, the achievement of business goals, or—more generically—greater effectiveness or efficiency.

Learning is another potential outcome from coaching, and is at least as important as performance because, taking a longer-term view, the future performance of the organization depends on it. The distinction I would make between that and **development** is that while you have to learn in order to develop, learning as I am using here refers to a broad domain—how to approach a task, getting to grips with new technology—while development is about personal growth and greater self-awareness.

Then I come to **facilitating**. Here it means more than simply to make things easier, although that is desirable too. To facilitate implies that the person being coached has the capacity to think something through for himself; the capacity to have an insight or creative idea. It acknowledges that people can learn without being taught. This in turn means that the coach has to give up on the fact that he has the right answer. The role of the coach is to enable the player to explore: to gain a better understanding, to become more aware, and from that place to make a better decision than he or she would have made previously. (I am aware that I am repeating myself a little here, and I apologize if this is an interference, but I think this is an idea that bears repetition.)

That leaves **art**. I do not mean to suggest that there is no science to coaching, for there is, and it forms much of the content of this book. Coaching is an art in the sense that when practised with excellence, there is no attention on the technique: the coach is fully engaged with the player, and the process of coaching becomes a dance between two people moving in complete harmony and partnership. At this point, the intelligence, intuition, and imagination of the coach become valuable contributions—rather than creating interference for the player.

The science of coaching comes out of experience and observations shared with like-minded people over a number of years and supported by other, related disciplines such as psychology or philosophy. Much of this book is devoted to a description of that science, but you should know that the science of coaching is not coaching. If you get stuck in doing it by the book, you are truly stuck, for your attention is simply with the 'right' way of doing it, and not with the player. Someone once said of acting that 'there are no rules, but you've got to know them'. Coaching is a bit like that.

The spectrum of coaching skills

A further part of the school's definition is the spectrum of coaching skills. Coaching is a relationship, and the conversation that takes place within that relationship can take a number of forms depending on the situation and the needs of the player.

The diagram below lays out most of the different conversational approaches a coach might take during a coaching session. The most important distinction made in the diagram is between directing and following interest. This builds on the observations I made in the previous section, about facilitation.

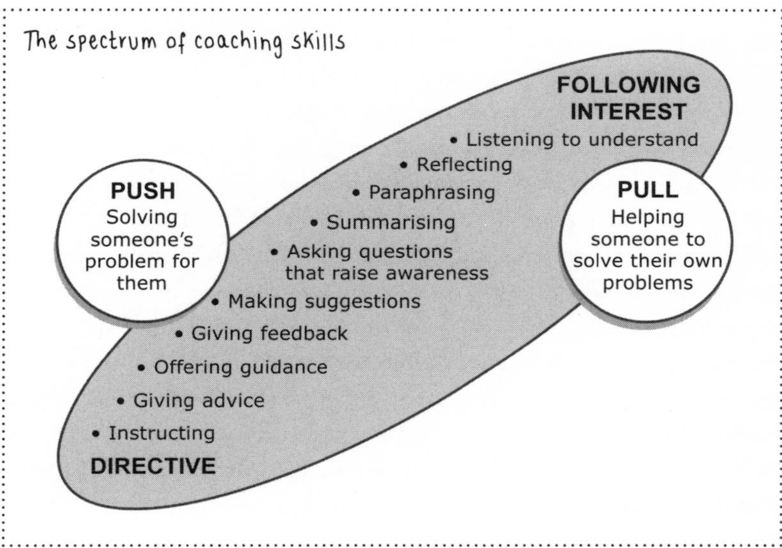

Directing means just that: to direct, to tell, to instruct. It is the form of education and management that we are most familiar with. Teacher knows, and—like it or not—will tell you. You, on the other hand, sit there, passively. The assumption is that once you have been told, you will know. And if you did not get it the first time around, the teacher merely has to increase the volume—because, as everyone knows, there is a direct correlation between understanding and volume.

There is an in-built limitation in the directive approach, which is that the coach has to know the answer already, or has to be able to work it out. Given the ways most organizations are structured, however, with so many people with different specialisms and unique issues reporting to a line manager, this is an unrealistic proposition. Surprisingly, the fact that we do not know the answer does not seem to stop some of us.

Occasionally, as part of a training programme to develop coaching skills, I take the participants onto the tennis court. The purpose of this is to get them to deepen the facilitation skills of following interest, the theory being that if they do not know the techniques involved in playing tennis, they cannot resort to instructions. What baffles me is that participants who have never played tennis before will still try to tell others how to play. It seems that the directive modelling of those early years is so very powerful that people are trapped in 'teaching' and do not see that teaching, frequently, has little to do with learning. On the other hand, what is amazing—and it amazes me every time I see it—is the results these coaches achieve when they adopt an approach based on following interest. People learn in minutes things that would take a traditional coach, operating from a more conventional model, hours to teach. (Or, rather, minutes to teach—forever to get across!)

In **following interest** you do not direct, instruct, or tell. Let me remind you how you learnt to walk. You learnt to walk through direct experience—a kind of trial and error. You stood up, and you had a go. You fell over. Unconsciously, your body–mind processed the information gained from that experience, took account of the results, and made the appropriate corrections. Most of us walk reasonably well, but few have had any direct instruction in how to do it.

Let me also tell what did not happen when you learnt to walk. A willing parent did not stand behind you, armed with *The Book That Has Been Handed Down Through the Ages,* and issue a series of instructions: 'Good boy. Now put all your weight on your right leg. OK. Let your left leg swing forward. Try to get some balance with your arms, no, stupid, your left leg.' You get the picture. Nor were there recriminations, punishments, or blame when you got it wrong. Parents in the early days are blessed with a non-judgmental approach that encourages experimentation and playfulness. And then, somewhere along the way, we—as parents, teachers, and managers—forget this. As I have said, each one of us is born with an innate capacity to learn—a sort of learning instinct, if you will. An effective coach seeks to tap into that instinct so that the player learns for himself.

Despite my passionate insistence about the limitations of a directive or 'tell' approach, it is important to understand that the directive end of the spectrum is also available to you as a coach. There will be times when you do know the answer, and the player is stuck. There will be times when your player needs some feedback or advice. In these situations, to withhold an answer would not be helpful. However, genius mostly emerges from the other end of the spectrum.

Effective coaching: the proposition

I suggested in the previous chapter that one way through the apparent confusion about coaching would be to let the ends define the means.

Effective coaching in the workplace delivers achievement, fulfilment, and joy from which both the individual and the organization will benefit. By **achievement**, I mean the delivery of extraordinary results: organizational and individual goals achieved; strategies, projects, and plans executed. It suggests effectiveness, creativity, and innovation. Effective coaching delivers achievement, which is sustainable. Because of the emphasis on learning, and because the confidence of the player is enhanced ('I worked it out for myself!'), the increase in performance is typically sustained for a longer period, and will impact on areas that were not directly the subject of the coaching.

In **fulfilment** I include learning and development. To achieve the business result is one thing; to achieve it in such a way that the player learns and develops as part of the process has a greater value—to the player, the line manager or coach, and the organization, for it is the capacity to learn that ensures an organization's survival.

I also include here the notion that work can be meaningful; that individuals through coaching begin to identify goals that are intrinsically rewarding. With fulfilment comes an increase in motivation. That the coach respects the player, his ideas, and his opinions; that the player is doing his work in his own way; that he is pursuing his own goals and is responsible—all of this makes for a player who is inspired and committed. In this way, more of the energy, intelligence, and imagination of each individual is brought to the service of the organization.

And **joy**. When people are achieving their goals—when those goals have some meaning, and when learning and developing is part of the process—enjoyment ensues. These three components—achievement, fulfilment, and joy—are interlinked, and the absence of any one of the three will impact on and erode the others. Learning without achievement quickly exhausts one's energy. Achievement without learning soon becomes boring. The absence of joy erodes the human spirit.

There is one other factor that I cannot fit neatly into the three outputs of effective coaching, but that lies implicitly behind them all: **responsibility**. Without responsibility and a sense of ownership, organizations quickly become ineffective.

Coaching directly and immediately impacts on responsibility. If the manager or coach solves the problem or decides on a course of action for the player, he has taken ownership and responsibility. Should the player hit an obstacle, he will come back to the manager or coach for more guidance. When the player defines his own goals, solves a problem for himself, or develops his own plan, the result is that responsibility stays with the player.

These ends—achievement, fulfilment, and joy—cannot be delivered through an approach in which the manager or coach instructs others as a function of their expertise, their knowledge, or—worse still—their status or authority. A wholly directive approach reduces the opportunity for the player to think or be creative, limits the possibility of their taking responsibility, and takes any satisfaction or joy out of what limited achievement there might be. Effective coaching, as described above, requires an approach in which the coach is intent on enabling the player to evoke genius; in which learning is intrinsic, and satisfaction derives from the pursuit and achievement of meaningful goals.

– CHAPTER 4 –

The effective coaching model

Not non-directive

In the previous editions of this book, I referred to 'non-directive coaching' and described my approach in those terms. Many people—both managers and coaches—have adopted a non-directive approach and it is understood by many organizations that use coaching to be a core concept.

The term 'non-directive' is most closely associated with Carl Rogers, an American psychologist who was deeply involved in the humanistic movement. Interestingly, the words were later dropped and replaced by 'client-centred' or 'person-centred'. 'Non-directive' is taken to mean that the coach does not direct the player—that is to say, he does not tell, advise, or suggest.

That is good as far as it goes, but it is more subtle than that. The question is this: who or what is being—or not being—directed? This is normally taken to mean the player. But what this is really about is the player's attention: what he is focusing on or thinking about in the moment of being coached. As a coach, you are looking to help the player choose what he pays attention to.

There are, however, at least three problems in calling coaching non-directive. The first problem is the obvious one: it tells you what *not* to do but not what to do—which, one has to acknowledge, is not very helpful. In only telling you *not* to do what every other learning or performance-related intervention has indicated you should do—to tell, or to teach— it almost creates a vacuum. Later on in this book, I will backfill this emptiness. Listening is key, but there is a way of asking questions that I call 'following interest'—the player's, not the coach's—that is at the absolute heart of effective coaching.

The second problem is that, in my view, an entirely non-directive approach is not what is most effective. Imagine a professional business coach in a coaching session; as the session comes to an end, the player has not come up with a viable way forward. Now, this coach has lots of experience of people in similar circumstances, and he has an insight. In my world, the coach does not simply get up and leave. That the coach would withhold an insight or knowledge would be unthinkable. We will talk about how a coach might make a suggestion later in the book when we discuss the skill set called 'proposing' (the title says it all, really).

The third problem is that it is impossible to be completely and utterly non-directive. If a player says something that I, the coach, either approve or disapprove of, this will be communicated, no matter how hard I try not to do so, and it will impact their thinking. We, as human beings, are designed to pick up even the most subtle signals, consciously or unconsciously: A half-smile, a flicker of the eyes, a change in breathing or facial colour—these things are all signals, all communications. The player will pick them up, and will almost certainly be influenced by them.

I will come back to this in the section on proposing. For the moment, let me simply say that in the effective coaching model, the coach might use his own experience, knowledge, insight, imagination—in short, his own resources—in service of the player, while being primarily reliant on the player's resources in their process of becoming unstuck and being successful.

The effective coaching model

In an early attempt to find a way to describe this approach, some colleagues and I acknowledged that there are resources in both the player and in the coach. This may seem obvious, but as I have said before, coaches can get precious and miss the obvious. Resources are all the qualities, characteristics, skills, and abilities a person is born with, as well as those he or she develops over time. They might include knowledge, experience, wisdom, imagination, intuition, and problem-solving. We referred to the resources in the player as 'over there' and to those in the coach as 'over here'. This proved a useful guide for people learning to coach—it allows the coach to ask himself the question: 'Whose resources are at work now, mine or the player's?' This corresponds well with the question suggested earlier: 'Over whose head is the thinking-bubble?'

The effective coaching model

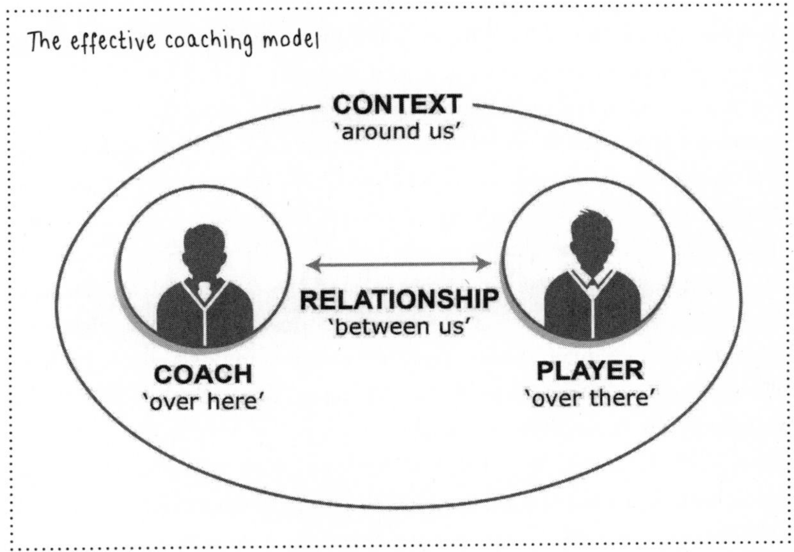

The player and coach are two of the four elements present in coaching. The other two are the relationship between the coach and the player (between us) and the context (around us). The relationship element (between us) has two main aspects: contracting and dynamics. **Contracting** is about making agreements, typically prior to beginning working together, to ensure a successful coaching relationship (see page xx.) **Dynamics** are the things that occur in the relationship: how the player sees the coach, how the coach sees the player, and how these perceptions change and develop over time.

This is not so much about 'chemistry'. There are those involved in coaching who hold the view that chemistry is a crucial component; for some professional coaches, the first meeting with a possible player is often described as a 'chemistry meeting'. I am not quite so convinced—a properly trained coach with a dash of self-awareness and a pinch of professionalism will typically generate a relationship fairly easily. The simple act of listening to the player and suspending judgment—core coaching skills, after all—are fundamental to building relationship. A far more critical factor in effective coaching is whether the player has a real and present need or aim that requires the support of another to be satisfied. I suggest therefore that it is more about developing and managing a healthy relationship than about a slightly mysterious thing called chemistry.

The **context** (around us) is often the forgotten element in coaching—forgotten, perhaps, because the coach is mostly so focused on the player and their story that other apparently peripheral things are left unattended. And yet, to borrow the phrase, 'context is king': it shapes our views, defines what is thought possible or permissible, and is the carrier of meaning. Context, with regard to coaching people in business, might include the organization's strategy, policies, culture, and stakeholders, the economic climate or other market conditions, and so on. (Clearly, this is potentially an endless list, so I will stop here.)

If I reflect on the coaching engagements that I have undertaken and look at those that have ether failed or been less than successful, it is most often something from outside that has been the obstacle—not something going on 'over there', not something 'over here', not something 'between us'.

A few years ago, I was working with a very senior director in a bank. He was referred to me because his performance had not been as expected; he was not showing the right leadership qualities, and his attitude, I was informed, was 'grumpy'. He and I worked hard together, but we were not really making any progress. Then it dawned on me—the CEO and HR director were unsure about whether they wanted to keep him on or get rid of him. They were keeping him on because it was a very fast-changing environment and most of the senior people were new to the business. My 'player' was one of the few who knew the business in depth. Unfortunately, he had a meaningless role that changed regularly, making it difficult to demonstrate high performance; a team that changed with each shift in role, making it difficult to demonstrate leadership; and he simply did not quite fit in with his new colleagues. So it was understandable that he was 'grumpy'.

Almost all of the obstacles to his being successful were contextual, so focusing the coaching on his leadership behaviours was paying no dividends. The situation was only resolved through a rather direct meeting with the HR director and the CEO which caused them to reflect on whether they truly wanted the director in the business. Interestingly, the answer was no—which, in this case, led to a positive outcome for all parties.
Each of these elements has a specific skill set attached to it, used to either exploit, manage, or understand it. These skills are shown below:

> OVER THERE includes what we might previously have described as the non-directive skills; keeping the thought-bubble over the player's head; listening, asking questions for clarity, asking questions that follow interest, summarizing.
>
> OVER HERE breaks into two elements: managing oneself and proposing. Managing oneself includes awareness of self in the moment (that is, an emotional response), clarity of intent, and boundary awareness, Proposing includes giving feedback, making suggestions, giving advice, challenging, and evoking creativity.
>
> BETWEEN US includes the skills of creating a contract, understanding and managing the relationship, transposition (putting yourself in the others shoes), and self-awareness.
>
> AROUND US is about taking a perspective almost as an external consultant might do. It includes the critical skills of generating and testing hypotheses.

Coaching from ...

As I have already noted, the effective coaching model is not a non-directive model, but it does borrow from that approach. One can coach from each of four main positions:

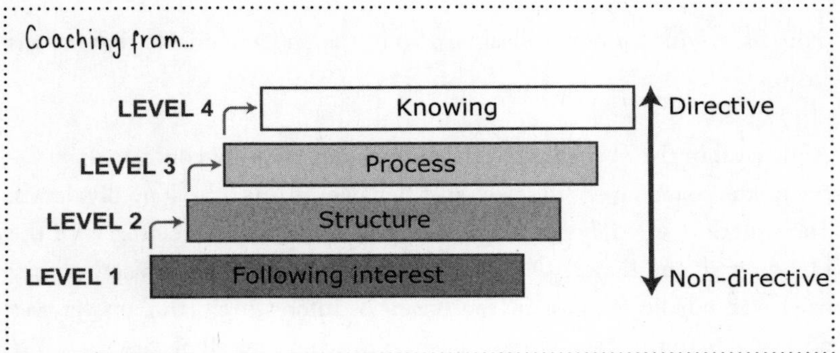

One can coach from **knowing**. Knowing is my knowledge; understanding that comes from my experience, my intuition, or my capacity to think. And I can coach from this place. The skill, of course, is to make sure that the coaching is relevant, and that the player is able and willing to hear it.. I frequently teach the leadership/management/coaching model described in chapter 11, as it is critical to understanding how to balance empowerment with appropriate control. I know it, they don't, so I teach it. And that is part of coaching.

One can also coach from **process**. In this context, a process is a sequence of instructions delivered by the coach that takes the player on a journey. An example of this might be a guided visualization.

One can also coach from **structure**. By structure, I mean the fundamental parts from which something is made up. There is a structure in time: past, present, and future. In a coaching session, if a player says that last year was the worst year of his life, coaching from a temporal structure allows the coach to ask how the player desires the next year to be.

The idea of **opposites** provides another structure. If something is bad, what does good look like? If there is a negative attitude—not caring, for instance—what is its opposite?

There are also many other models the coach might find it useful to follow. In chapter 15, you will find a model called the pillars of enabling genius (drive, identity, mindset, learning), which a coach could use to help a player identify areas for development.

One can also coach from **following interest**. I asserted earlier that it is impossible to be completely non-directive. Following interest is as close to being non-directive as you can get. It keeps the thought-bubble firmly over the player's head, and is designed to help players choose where to direct their attention, what they want to think about. This is a critical skill and one that I will describe it in greater detail in part two of this book.
The diagram above shows the more directive skills at the top and the non-directive at the bottom. In effective coaching, I am suggesting that following interest is the core skill set. If a person cannot do this, in my view, he should simply not put himself forward as a coach.

Thinking unfolds

Some years back, I was flying into Austin, Texas, and as the plane began its descent I was looking out of the window. I had been thinking about thinking, my mind slightly adrift after a long flight. I noticed the river below, taking long sweeping turns to the left and right as it made its way out to the sea. And it struck me that one could look at that river with an engineer's mind: to notice the waste of time and energy in those meanderings and decide that the obvious thing to do would be to build a canal in one straight line, direct from source to sea.

Something was knocking on the door of my consciousness. But then, I thought, the river was following a straight line—just not one you can see from 35,000 feet. At ground level—if you could get far enough away to see it—you would see that the river flowed in a pretty straight line, from high to low. And you might also notice that it was taking the path of least resistance. Almost as if the water had its own logic.

Back to thinking. What if our capacity to think had its own internal logic? What if *thinking unfolds*? If only we would trust our thinking—trust the process, the unfolding.

Then I thought about a dear friend of mine who has struggled with depression for most of her life. Every now and then she would seek help, both medical intervention and 'talking therapies'. With the latter, I noticed a pattern: the first two or three session would be productive and useful, but by the third or fourth the value and enthusiasm would start to diminish. My hypothesis is this: in the early sessions, the therapist or counsellor *has* to listen—he does not know the client! There would be value as my friend told her story, allowing her thinking to unfold, meandering as required, and make its way toward the sea. But come the third or fourth session, the therapist would have formed an opinion, taken a position, and begun to propose a way forward. Let's build a canal! At that point, the thinking can no longer unfold.

– CHAPTER 5 –

Effective coaching and mindset

One of the threads in this book that you will probably have picked up is the idea of mindset or mental state. There is a mindset in which we perform to our best and learn most effectively. I first learnt about this as a competitive tennis player, noticing that there was a mental state in which I played my best tennis. Gallwey called is 'self two'; Carol Dweck (whose work I'll refer to in detail later) called it a 'growth mindset'. This is fundamental to learning and performance, and therefore is key to the effective coaching model.

A golf lesson

It's a cold, wet, and windy autumnal day in the south of England. And it's early. I am at a driving range, waiting for Patrick, the CEO of a large engineering company, who is interested in finding out about my approach to coaching and the influence of the 'inner game'. He arrives, and I discover that he has his HR director with him. We are introduced as he takes his clubs from the car and make our way to the end bay in the range. I get him to loosen up by hitting a few balls. He plays golf about ten times a year, he says, mostly for business reasons, and has had a few lessons.

'Which part of your game are you most interested in improving?' I ask. Patrick looks at the clubs in his bag, hesitates, and then says: 'My driving. I don't seem to be able to get the length that others do. And I tend to slice it.'

I put a ball on the tee in front of him. 'Show me.'

Patrick hits the ball. Sure enough, it begins to turn to the right and just about reaches the 150-yard marker. He hits another ball, and the result is much the same.

'Is that what you'd expect?'

He nods his head. 'Yes. I am not very coordinated, and I have always avoided sports of any kind. I only play because some of my clients like to do business on the golf course. And it's worse with clients, because they're all watching you perform.'

'Right. If we were to be really successful here, what kind of shot would you be hitting at the end of the session?'

'I guess the ball would bounce just beyond the 175-yard marker, and would be fairly straight.'

'How would we know that it was straight?'

'It would be between those trees to the right on the horizon and the electricity pylon. In that corridor.'

'OK. Here's what I want you to do. First, don't worry about the goal for the moment. Forget about it, in fact. We'll come back to it later. Now, I want you to hit a few balls and simply tell me what you notice.'

'How do you mean?'

'Try this. Stand on one foot and put all your attention into the foot on the ground. Exactly. What do you notice?'

'It's balancing.'

'That is not what you notice. That is what you think about—a concept. There's a world of difference. Tell me what you actually notice.'

'It's wobbling.'

'Be more precise.'

'The foot is moving from side to side.'

'Is there anything else?'

'I can feel my weight over the front of my foot, over the ball.'

'Now, what I want you to do is to hit a golf ball and to simply notice what you are doing.'

Patrick hits a few balls. 'I am noticing my hips moving, coming through too early.'

'Too early?'

'That's what the pro tells me.'

'Fine, but don't worry about that for the moment. Hit a few more and tell me what you notice this time.'

'I noticed that I did not make good contact on the last two, and there's something else: the stroke feels a bit funny.'

'Funny?'

'Yes, more … it's kind of jerky.'

'You've noticed three things: your hips, the contact between the ball and the club, and this jerky business. Hit some more and tell me which is the most interesting. What stands out?'

Patrick hits a few more balls.

'The jerkiness.'

'Hit a few more, and don't try to change anything. Tell me where exactly in the stroke it feels jerky.'

Patrick hits some more. 'It's in the downswing.'

'All through the downswing, or just a bit of it?'

He hits another ball. 'It's in the second half of the downswing.'

'Great. Hit another, and tell me where it is this time.'

'Interesting. That one was just in the last quarter.'

'Hit another.'

'Amazing.'

'What is?'

'There's no jerkiness there.'

'If there's no jerkiness, what do you notice in its place?'

Patrick hits some more. He's smiling now. 'Fluidity.'

'Tell me after the next stroke how fluid it was. Use a scale of one to ten.'

He hits a ball. 'About five.' Another ball. 'Hmm. More.'

'Where's more on a scale of one to ten?'

'Six. Maybe seven.'

Another ball. 'Seven.' Another. 'Eight.'

The HR director has started laughing. Patrick looks up, mild surprise showing on his face. If he had not been so engrossed in noticing the fluidity quotient of his stroke, he would have noticed that the ball was consistently flying straight and well past the 175 yard marker.

The lesson with Patrick is typical of many golf lessons I have given. If you go back through the script, you will notice that I have not given one technical instruction. There are two reasons for this: one is that, as I have already explained, most instruction does not help people learn. The second is that I don't play golf, and therefore could not give a technical instruction even if I wanted to. But the golf coaching that I give is pretty successful. I am drawing your attention to this again because I really want you to appreciate that the coach's primary job is to help the player get into the right mindset—relaxed concentration, or flow. And you do not have to know very much about the discipline or topic in order to help someone learn—it's hard-wired, and it kicks in when the mindset is right.

I want to remind you that the concepts described in this chapter are my interpretation of the inner game. Imagine my shock and nervousness when I was delivering a session at a conference in Amsterdam, and Tim Gallwey—whom I had met for the first time the evening before—silently took a seat at the back. I was concerned then that what I was presenting was congruent with his ideas, and in writing this chapter now, I am experiencing a similar thing, so let me be clear about my intentions. There are elements of the inner game that I have 'made my own', and that fit particularly well with the notions of effective coaching. In this chapter, I want to present my understanding of the principles and some of the most relevant techniques, and relate some more recent research in support of those principles.

The first lesson or distinction that we are offered is in the name: the inner game. Inner implies outer. If you have ever had conventional golf tuition, you will hear three things at the end: 'That will be $50 please', 'Keep practising', and 'It's all in the mind'. The sequence of the statements is very important (to the pro). He knows he must ask for and get the money before making the last statement because otherwise—given that it is 'all in the mind', and the pro has done nothing to address the mind—no self-respecting client would pay up.

I do not mean to malign golf pros, however. Most conventional tuition addresses the outer game—the techniques, the grips, the stance, the physical movement. This is understandable, as it is both visible and measurable. The contents of the inner game, on the other hand, are more elusive, and they cannot be observed or measured. These are things like perception, aspirations, values, fears, and doubts. The models and techniques presented here offer an approach to addressing the inner game.

In chapter 2 I introduced one of the key models in the inner game—potential minus interference is equal to performance—and suggested that the role of the coach is to reduce the interference, thus releasing more of the potential of the player. In the opening golf lesson, Patrick exhibited a few fine examples of the type of interference I mean:

> 'Yes. I am not very coordinated, and I have always avoided sports of any kind. I only play because some of my clients like to do business on the golf course. And it's worse with clients, because they're all watching you perform.'

Fear and doubt. Nothing interferes more with human performance. Fear and doubt fuel the outer game as we try to find the 'right' way to swing the club or deliver a presentation, and thus create a self-perpetuating loop. Out of the fear that we may get it wrong, we try to identify the 'right' way—the right approach or technique. We then try to execute this right way, and this in turn becomes an interference, engendering more fear and doubt.

The tennis player Ivan Lendl had numerous coaches (most of whom got fired) who tried to teach him their own unique 'right' way to hit a forehand. Lendl ultimately found his way, which was somewhat unconventional for the time—and the rest is history.

The following anecdote is a slight diversion, but it is indicative of how invasive and constricting fear and doubt can be. I attended an event recently where half a dozen or so 'captains of industry' were present. One of them started talking about the need for creativity in his organization. A number of the others had a similar need. Within two minutes, the conversation had turned to risk management. The message that they were communicating to the staff was something like: 'I want more creativity, but don't make a mistake.' And they were wondering why there was so little creativity in their organization!

Interference is the prime obstacle to performance. On a Sunday night many years ago, when my stepdaughter Victoria was about 11 years old, and on her way to bed, I asked whether all her homework had been completed. Her face fell; there was an English essay outstanding, and she had to do it that night. Having just sat down to finish a bottle of wine, I was not entirely delighted when my offer of help was accepted. We sat down side by side at the kitchen table. I asked what the topic of the essay was and wrote it down at the top of the page. I then asked for her thoughts on the topic.

Victoria knew the game well enough by this stage and understood that I was not going to write the essay but rather help her marshal her thoughts and get started. Knowing her to be very bright and full of ideas, I was a little surprised and, yes, agitated when she didn't answer. I turned to her with the intent of asking the question again—with more energy—when I noticed that she had curled up in the chair with her feet under her in a manner that still causes me to wonder at the flexibility of the human body. If her face had fallen earlier, this time it turned white as well. My agitation disappeared.

'What's up?' I asked.

'The essay should have been in on Friday, and it's the third time that I have been late. Miss White is the only teacher who believes in me, and now I've let her down and, and ...'

'I see. What can you do about it?'

'Nothing.'

'Nothing?'

After a little while, we got to: 'If I finished the essay and got it to her first thing in the morning, and said sorry, maybe she won't be so cross with me, and I would not have to sit through the whole morning worrying about the English class in the afternoon.'

'OK. Are you ready to do the essay?'

'Yes.'

'Tell me, what thoughts do you have about this topic?'

There followed a torrent of ideas. I jotted them down and read them back to her. Could she see a structure, a storyline? Yes. What more help did she need? I was to go away and let her finish. There was still an inch of wine.

The two selves

When a person is focused, and the interference—or most of it—is removed, he enters into a different mental state sometimes called flow. Gallwey had a particular view on this, which he describes in The Inner Game of Tennis, and which is very valuable. He noticed the capacity of people to have a conversation with themselves; you can hear such conversations everyday, everywhere, but they are perhaps most evident in the sporting arena.

These conversations are notable for the criticism, judgment, and condemnation that people heap upon themselves. There then typically follows a set of instructions about how to do whatever the task is better:

> 'You idiot, you know you should hit the ball in front of you.'
> 'You're so lazy!'
> 'Stay on your toes and get the racket back early.'

'Who is talking to whom?' Gallwey asked. He answers his own question thus: 'Obviously, the who and the whom are separate entities or there would be no conversation, so that one could say that within each player there are two "selves". One … seems to give instructions; the other … seems to perform the action. Let's call the "teller" Self One and the "doer" Self Two.'

I describe self one and self two as follows:

> SELF ONE is the internalized voice of our parents, teachers, and those in authority. Self one seeks to control self two and does not trust it. Self one is characterized by tension, fear, doubt, and trying too hard.
>
> SELF TWO is the whole human being, with all its potential and capacities including the hard-wired capacity to learn. It is characterized by relaxed concentration, enjoyment, and trust.

On workshops, I will often ask people to describe moments when they have experienced self two. The first people to speak are usually those who engage in sport—skiing is a big one—followed by those who play music or sing. Then come the writers and the artists, until everyone in the room can identify a time when they have been 'in flow'. As the conversation progresses, more and more situations are identified, including those that take place at work; writing a difficult report, a presentation, a sales meeting. In any moment—in any situation—you have the opportunity to be in either self one or self two.

This has relevance here for three reasons:

- As a coach, your intention must be to operate from self two. This is where you will do your best and most rewarding work. I will talk about this in chapter 16.
- When you are coaching, the intent is also to help players get into—and stay in—self two. In this way, they can do their best thinking and be the most objective, insightful, intuitive, and creative they can be.
- Helping players to be in self two in everyday life—and particularly in the critical moments, such as key meetings and presentations—is part of the coach or line manager's role.

Fixed and growth mindset

Gallwey formed his 'inner game' model out of his direct, day-to-day experience as both a coach and a player of tennis—there was no scientific research behind it. That was back in 1974. Today, there is a significant amount of research, with much understanding gained and many papers published on performance and learning.

One concept that broadly supports Gallwey's concept of the two selves is Carol Dweck's notion of 'mindset'. Dweck is a highly regarded professor of psychology at Stanford University. In her book Mindset, she talks about how her research over a period of 20 years has shown how 'the view you adopt for yourself profoundly affects the way you lead your life'. In a sense that's to no real surprise, but as we will see later, in the chapter on genius, this gives us significant choice as to what we become.

Dweck goes on introduce the idea that there are two distinctly different mindsets: a fixed mindset and a growth mindset. As I understand it, a fixed mindset is wrapped around a core belief that your abilities are 'carved in stone'—all you have is what you were born with, and there's nothing you can do about it. This can manifest itself in two very different ways: a need to prove oneself over and over again, or simply to give up.

The need to prove oneself over and over again can be seen in so many people in so many walks of life, and is so very destructive. As Dweck puts it: 'If you have only a certain amount of intelligence, a certain personality, and a certain moral character—well then, you had better prove that you have a healthy dose of them. It certainly wouldn't do to look deficient in these most basic characteristics.'

And then there are those who simply seem to have given up. The story goes a bit like this: 'I was never any good at anything, so it's not worth making the effort. I am the way I am.'

The growth mindset is based on the belief that your basic qualities are things you can cultivate through your efforts. In reading Dweck's book, I have also understood that one's mindset can show up in two different ways: as a life-long position, as a way of relating to oneself, or as an 'in the moment' experience. I can be giving a speech at a conference—something I really enjoy doing—and doubt can rear up, apparently out of nowhere. 'They're not enjoying this,' I think. 'I should have prepared more.' I lose my way a little, becoming less clear and forgetting what I am to say next. As a player of the inner game, I can usually find my way back to a growth mindset, or my self two. That's a skill that can be learned. But you have to know about it first.

Following interest

There is no guaranteed method of getting into self two, but I believe one of the keys to it is on what Gallwey called 'relaxed concentration'. This mental state—where the player is focused, relaxed, and trusting—is another way of describing self two.

The continuum of attention

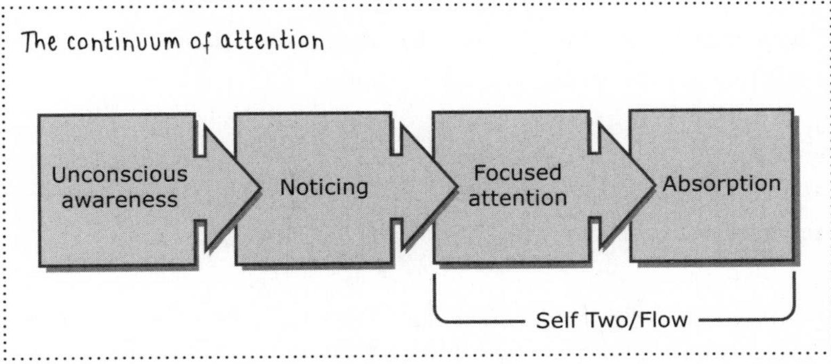

Let me suggest that there is a kind of continuum of attention. It starts with what I call 'unconscious awareness', where things are happening but you are not consciously paying attention to them. As we move across the continuum we get to 'noticing', which is where you become conscious of what is in your attention, either as a function of choice or because it is compelling. Then there is 'focused attention', and finally 'absorption', where there is nothing else on your mind but the focus on the activity. On the right-hand side of the continuum, you will tend to be in self two or flow—the state in which you will perform and/or learn most effectively and enjoyably.

One approach that a coach might use to help a player move across the continuum is **following interest**. This is the fundamental skill of effective coaching, and is what makes a 'non-directive' approach work. Let me take a snippet from the golf lesson described earlier: Patrick's response to my question about what he noticed.

'I am noticing my hips moving, coming through too early.'

'Too early?'

'That's what the pro tells me.' *(Possibility for interference, judgment.)*

'Fine, but don't worry about that for the moment.' *(Removing interference.)* 'Hit a few more and tell me what you notice this time.'

'I noticed that I did not make good contact on the last two, and there's something else: the stroke feels a bit funny.'

'Funny?'

'Yes, more … it's kind of jerky.'

'You've noticed three things: your hips, the contact between the ball and the club, and this jerky business. Hit some more and tell me which is the most interesting. What stands out?' *(Focusing by following interest; using the Model T, as described in chapter 6.)*

'The jerkiness.'

'Hit a few more, and don't try to change anything.' *(Avoiding possible interference; trying to get it right.)* 'Tell me where exactly in the stroke it feels jerky.' *(Focusing attention.)*

Patrick hits some more. 'It's in the downswing.'

'All through the downswing, or just a bit of it?'

He hits another ball. 'It's in the second half of the downswing.'
'Great. Hit another and tell me where it is this time.'

'Interesting. That one was just in the last quarter.'

'Hit another.'

'Amazing.' *(Self two/absorption; there is no judgment in 'amazing', just pleasure and awe.)*

'What is?'

'There's no jerkiness there.'

'If there's no jerkiness, what do you notice in its place?'

Patrick hits some more. He's smiling now. 'Fluidity.'

'Tell me after the next stroke how fluid it was. Use a scale of one to ten.'

He hits a ball. 'About five.' Another ball. 'Hmm. More.'

Here, following interest involves this basic process:

- 'Tell me what you notice.'
- 'Tell me what else you notice.'
- 'Of all the things you have noticed, which is most interesting?'
- 'Tell me some more about that which is most interesting.'

This idea helped me develop the Model T, which I describe in full in chapter 6. a little more. The horizontal bar of the T—'expand'—is driven by noticing questions, and the vertical bar—'focus'—is driven by interest.

In his book *Focus: The Hidden Driver of Excellence* (the title says it all), Daniel Goldman suggests that there are 'several doorways to flow. One may open when we tackle a task that challenges our abilities to the maximum—a "just manageable" demand on our skills. Another entryway can come via doing what we are passionate about; motivation sometimes drives us into flow. But either way the final common pathway is full focus: these are each ways to ratchet up attention. No matter how you get there, a keen focus jump-starts flow.'

'Awareness is curative'

Something else is happening while the coach is following the interest of the player, and helping him to focus (and thus into self two): the player is becoming more aware of what actually is happening, and as long as he does not try to analyze the data but simply notices and focuses on it, the natural process of learning will kick in.

The title of this section is a quote from The Inner Game of Work that many find almost counterintuitive. I saw Gallwey work briefly with a woman some years back. She was a senior management consultant in what was one of the 'big five' accountancy practices, and she had a problem with anxiety when faced with very senior clients, such as CEOs. The conversation went something like this:

> TIM: How anxious do you get, say on a scale of one to ten?
> WOMAN: About seven or eight.
> TIM: Will you be meeting anyone with whom you might get anxious in the next few weeks?

The woman identified two or three such meetings.

> TIM: What I suggest is that you rate your anxiety on a scale of 1 to 10 just before, during and after the meetings.

End of conversation. Awareness is curative.

A key part of becoming aware is the act—or is it the art?—of **noticing**. Noticing is without judgment, and is untainted by fear, doubt, aspiration, or wish. Noticing is the 'not trying' of thinking. It allows a person to take in a much broader band and quantity of data, and, as there is no judgment, eliminates interference. As I see it, this data is processed by self two and produces results effortlessly and elegantly that are often surprising.

After I sold the School of Coaching, I maintained a full-time involvement for about two years. During the process of integrating the school into a significantly bigger, global organization, I struggled to find my role—not least because we had appointed a managing director to run the business, and I did not want to get in the way of that. So I found it quite difficult to have an impact in the business.

With the help of a coach, I looked at my leadership style. One of the strategies that emerged from this was for me to become more aware, on an hour-to-hour basis, of my sense of 'inspiration'. I would rate this on a scale of one to ten but not necessarily do anything specific as a result.

On one particular morning, when I was about three minutes away from the office, I rated my sense of inspiration. It was three. As I entered the building, I caught the receptionist's eye. She asked whether I had been away, and in fact I had, so I told her a little of my trip. To my surprise, she thanked me and said that she really had no idea what went on in the building, because no one told her.

I continued on to my own office, where we had our own receptionist. She asked how my trip had been. I responded. She then thanked me and informed me that she only had a sketchy idea of what we all did, adding that it was really interesting to hear more about it.

Now, to get to my desk I had two options: to walk through the main office, or to take a back corridor. Being a shy and retiring type, I always took the back corridor. On this day, however, I found myself walking through the main office, greeting and being greeting by my colleagues. I enquired of one about a project he was working on, and we had a short but interesting chat about the options. As I moved on, my colleague thanked me, saying that it had been really inspirational.

That stopped me in my tracks. Without any effort, I had changed my behaviour, and had an entirely different level of impact. Awareness is indeed curative. In my current role, I spend a lot of time writing and creating. To keep myself focused and motivated, I rate my sense of selected qualities two or three times a day. These are usually flow, focus, and joy. The very act of bringing them to mind brings them into my work.

The player in self two

As noted earlier, one of the roles of the coach is to help the player move into self two through the processes of following interest and becoming focused. The coach should also be observing the player with a little detachment, noticing body language. It is useful too for the coach to ask himself the question: 'Is the player in self two?'

If the answer is no, a simple observation such as 'you look a little uncomfortable' can unlock the conversation. If a coaching conversation is stuck, look for the interference. It will be present—and it might be you. I recollect a coaching conversation with a partner in a large, international consultancy who had some understanding of the inner game. We were discussing his career vision and goals, and I confess I was close to falling off my chair with boredom. But this was a highly intelligent and creative man. So I asked him whether he was in self one or self two.

'Self one, I guess,' he replied.

'What would it take for you to get into self two?'

'I'd have to stand up.'

The answer surprised me a little.

'And what do I have to do?' I asked.

'You have to stand up, too.'

We started again, each of us walking around the room, and as you might imagine, the results were more exciting and challenging and more congruent with whom this player actually was.

I will often tell people I am working with about my understanding of these key inner game concepts because they become valuable tools for them to give their best performance in everyday life. For instance, I know that one of the quickest ways to self two is through enjoyment.

Let me give you an example of how this works. In my youth, I was a good tennis player, until injury stopped me from playing. Eventually, I had surgery on a damaged shoulder, and that corrected the problem. Soon after the rehabilitation process, I went to hit some tennis balls. I had not played for years, and I was unfit, but even so, I was surprised to find myself playing quite so badly. So, as a good apprentice in the inner game, I tried a drill to focus attention and get into self two. Boy, I tried! After a while, I was still playing appallingly, and I observed to myself that I was not enjoying it. Then it hit me—there must be some enjoyment in playing the game I love to play, and in realizing that the surgery had been a success. I rated my enjoyment as a three. I played another rally and rated myself again. Still three. Another rally, and this time the rating was five. And then sevens and eights.

As the enjoyment went up, so did the quality of my tennis. What is interesting in this is that you cannot make yourself enjoy something; awareness is curative, and in this case it transformed my performance. Now, when working with colleagues at conference or training programme, I will frequently ask, 'What is your level of enjoyment?' I will then notice a slightly anxious face relax into a smile.

Flow

I want to include some material here that does not come from the inner-game school but which serves to support those ideas while adding greatly to the overall understanding. This material comes from Mihaly Csikszentmihalyi (pronounced 'chick-sent-me-high-ee', I am told), professor of psychology at the University of Chicago. I would compare Gallwey's 'self two' with what Csikszentmihalyi calls 'flow'. His best-known book is *Flow: The Psychology of Happiness*, in which he describes how, 'in the flow state action follows upon action according to an internal logic that seems to need no conscious intervention by the actor'.

Daniel Goleman, too, refers to flow in his book *Emotional Intelligence:* 'Flow is a state of self-forgetfulness, the opposite of rumination and worry. People in flow exhibit a masterly control of what they are doing, their responses perfectly attuned to the changing demands of the task.' Later, he writes: 'People perform at their best in flow ... the sheer pleasure of the act itself is what motivates them.'

Csikszentmihalyi identifies the following conditions as pertaining to the flow experience:

- There are clear goals every step of the way.
- There is immediate feedback to one's actions.
- There is a balance between the challenges and the skills required.
- Action and awareness are merged.
- Distractions are excluded from consciousness.
- There is no worry of failure.
- Self-consciousness disappears.
- The activity becomes autotelic. (This comes from the Greek: auto means 'self' and *telos* means 'goal', suggesting that the activity itself is its own reward.)

In these conditions, you will be able to see clearly the idea of interference expressed in a different form. For instance, the absence of a clear goal and feedback creates immense interference. On their own, these conditions form a wonderful checklist by which you might organize your own work life and that of those you coach.

Postscript

In this chapter, I have tried to communicate the fundamental notion at work in effective coaching and above all to demonstrate the extraordinary capacity of human beings to perform, learn, and be creative. Human beings also have an extraordinary capacity to get in their own way and create interference for themselves. Let me give a final anecdote in this chapter. I was coaching the operations director of a medium-sized business who was trying to bring two parts of the business together into one unit.

BILL: The problem is that I can only see one way of doing it—and it's not very good. *(He described this 'one way', and he was right: it was not very good.)*
MYLES: Tell me how else you could do it.
BILL: I told you I'm not very creative.
MYLES: I know, but if you were creative, what would you come up with?

Bill looked at me and laughed. The atmosphere changed, and it was clear that I was not going to let him off the hook. It took another couple of minutes to identify three more options. Not creative? Nonsense.

The last word in this chapter should, I think, go to Gallwey: a quote from his book, *The Inner Game of Work*. I want to draw your attention to two words that he uses here. The first is 'mobility'. Not movement, but mobility—the capacity to move. What I read into this is that the choice to move rests with the player. The other word is 'caring', and I do not need to explain that.

> '[Coaching] … must be learned mostly from experience. In the Inner Game approach, coaching can be defined as the facilitation of mobility. It is the art of creating an environment, through conversation and a way of being, that facilitates the process by which a person can move towards desired goals in a fulfilling manner. It requires one essential ingredient that cannot be taught; caring not only for the external result but for the person being coached.'

MODELS AND SKILLS

– CHAPTER 6 –

The models of effective coaching

The GROW model

This chapter describes how to manage a coaching conversation. As will be obvious by now, you cannot manage the content of the conversation; that belongs to the player. To be effective when coaching, however, you need to manage yourself, and the structure and process of the session. The idea of managing yourself is addressed in chapter 16, 'The art of coaching', and is a lifelong journey. Being in control of the structure and the process is an easier game.

The GROW model

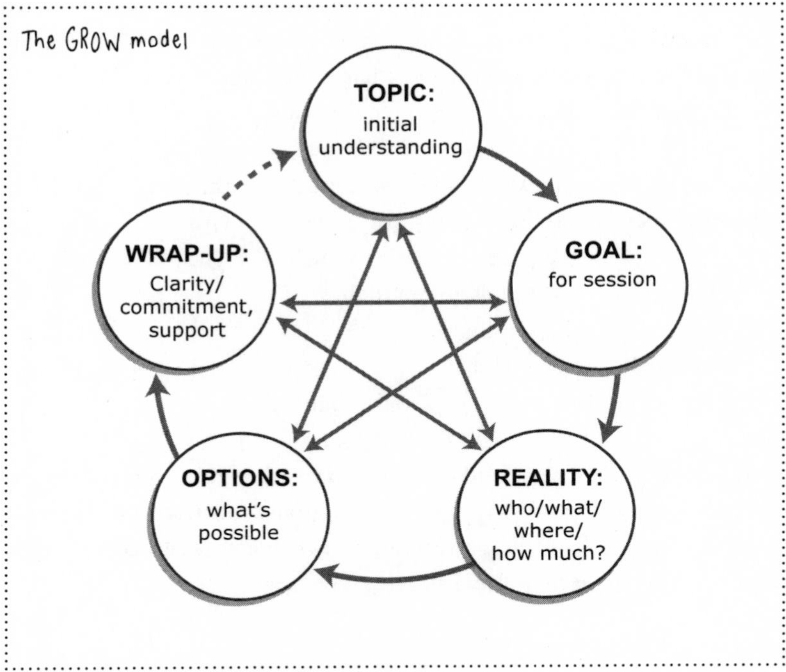

The GROW model (see diagram above) enables the manager or coach to structure a conversation and deliver a meaningful result. The practice of effective coaching was already in place before the GROW model was 'discovered', and the early practitioners of coaching worked more or less intuitively. Over time, it became apparent that in the more successful sessions there was a certain sequence of key stages, and these are source of the GROW model. The people who developed it were friends and colleagues of mine: Sir John Whitmore (author of *Coaching for Performance*), Graham Alexander, and Alan Fine.
The GROW model grew out of best practice and not theory. I tell you this because for many people, the first use of the model feels unnatural. You should know that once you have used it a few times, it begins to feel fluent, to the point where you hardly have to think of it, or refer to it only as a sort of checking point if the conversation is not going well.

The first letter of each stage in the model gives you GROW. Well, almost. What is missing is the first and rather critical stage: that of identifying the topic for the session. Attempts to include this stage in the mnemonic have been clumsy, however; the best suggestion was to call it the 'T GROW' model. In any case, it was too late to change the name, because by now the model had already gained considerable currency.

Imagine someone comes to you for some coaching. The sequence of questions that goes something like this:

> 'What do you want to talk to me about?'
> 'What's actually happening?'
> 'What could you do about it?'
> 'What are you definitely going to do about it?'

This would be an obvious and natural path to take, and covers four of the five elements of GROW: topic, reality, options, and wrap-up. The only missing element from the perspective of the model is the goal. Let me take you through each of these stages.

Topic

This is the first stage in any coaching conversation. At this point, a detailed account of the subject matter is not necessary. What you want is to understand the territory you are in, the scale of the topic, the importance and sometimes the emotional significance for the player. It is sometimes useful to establish what the player's longer-term vision or goal is. As the coach, you are looking for that moment when something inside you says: 'This is what they want to talk about.'

At the topic stage, the coach's intention is to understand what, specifically, the player wants to talk about:

COACH: What would you like to talk about?
PLAYER: As you know, I've got to make a presentation to the board next week, and I'm a bit nervous about doing a good job.
COACH: Tell me some more about that.
PLAYER: The team have asked me to make the presentation on Project Blue, and I am not at all sure how I should approach it.
COACH: Right.
PLAYER: And if I tell the truth, I'm a bit nervous about standing up before the board. They have a reputation for being tough on people who don't present well.
COACH: Yes, I know. Is there anything else about this?
PLAYER: Not really. Well, yes, the last time I made a presentation to a senior group it did not go very well.
COACH: Let me check. Is there a broader issue here about your presentation skills?
PLAYER: I guess so.
COACH: Specifically, then, what is the topic for the session?
PLAYER: It's about making a good presentation to the board, and also about improving my presentation skills in general.
COACH: If you could make progress with those skills, how would you want it to be?

Goal

While all the stages of the model are critical, the goal stage has perhaps the greatest impact on the success of the coaching conversation. In fact, 'goal' is not the best word to describe this stage. The coach is trying to establish the desired **outcome** for the conversation—something that will be achieved within the discussion itself. It is not the longer-term objective that the player has for the topic.

For example, a goal or vision to generate £400,000 of new sales in the next three months (which could not be achieved within the coaching conversation—unless it was a very long conversation!) is different from an outcome, which might be to have a strategy to deliver £400,000 of new sales in the next three months. So the outcome is the **strategy.**

When you are clear about that as the coach, you have a focus for the conversation. I have an image of this for myself: I have a tent on a beach with red and white stripes, rather Victorian, like a Punch & Judy stall.

Above the entrance is a sign that says: 'Your problems solved. $200 or your money back.' When my client enters, we establish a contract in the form of an **achievable outcome** for the coaching. I do not get paid unless that outcome is delivered. This outcome is typically an action step, a plan, a new idea, or simply to think an issue through. (The tent, just so you know, is somewhere warmer than the UK, otherwise the season would not be long enough to make a living.)

In the goal stage, the coach's intention is to identify and agree a clear and achievable outcome:

> COACH: OK, I think I've got a fair understanding of the topic. Tell me what you would like to get out of this session.
> PLAYER: Well, I'm more concerned about the immediate problem—the presentation to the board—than I am about reaching the longer-term thing—being happy to speak to groups of 50 or more. So I'd like to focus more on that.
> COACH: Fine. And tell me what you want from this session.
> PLAYER: Well, I'd like to understand what went wrong in the presentation to the senior managers that I mentioned, and then to have an idea of the key things to do differently next week.

COACH: There are two bits in that. To understand what went wrong and to have an idea of the key things to do differently. Take the first bit. What outcome would you want from understanding what went wrong?
PLAYER: To have identified the key lessons.
COACH: What does 'key' mean?
PLAYER: The most important. The two or three things that make or break a presentation.
COACH: And for the second bit? 'The key things to do differently.' What outcome would you like from that?
PLAYER: Obviously, the discussion about what went wrong may give me some of the things to do differently, but I suspect there are some other things that I need to know.
COACH: And the outcome?
PLAYER: If I could find in the whole session five or six key things to do or remember, that would be great.
COACH: So let me summarize where we've got to …

Reality

This stage of the model is concerned with achieving the most accurate picture of the topic possible. The coach encourages the player to discuss and become more aware of all aspects of the topic. In this phase, the primary function of the coach is to understand: not to solve, fix, heal, make better, or be wise, but to **understand**. No analysis, no problem solving, no wisdom, no good ideas, no jumping to conclusions. The magic is that it is in that moment of the coach understanding that the player understands for himself and becomes more aware—and is then in a position to make better decisions and choices than he would have done before.

In this stage, the coach's intention is to generate the clearest possible understanding of the topic:

COACH: You've mentioned the presentation that didn't work so well and then this other, more generic, 'other things you might do'. Are there any other elements to this?
PLAYER: Not that I can think of.
COACH: Which of the two do you want to tackle first?

PLAYER: I think the obvious place to start is with the presentation that I messed up.

COACH: OK. Tell me about that.

PLAYER: It was in an earlier stage of this project, and it was my turn to present—we take it in turns. I thought it was going to be relatively straightforward, but in the event it turned out all wrong.

COACH: Just how bad was it?

PLAYER: It wasn't a complete disaster, and they did get the message. It was that I really didn't do the work we had done—or myself—justice.

COACH: So what actually happened?

PLAYER: I was a bit flustered when I got there. We had worked late the night before, and at that point I thought I knew what I had to do. However, on the morning I felt unprepared. I was still putting the slides in order minutes before I was due to start.

COACH: What else happened?

PLAYER: Apart from not feeling prepared, I was really nervous, and my words came out a bit scrambled. At one point, someone asked me to repeat what I had just said because they had not understood.

COACH: Was there anything else in the session that did not work for you?

PLAYER: Yes. I was put out by a number of the questions. I don't think that anyone was trying to be difficult; I just found it difficult to find the answers.

COACH: So far in this conversation, you've mentioned something about your preparation, about feeling nervous, and the difficulty you had in answering questions. Is there anything else that you remember?

PLAYER: Not really. That's enough to work with.

COACH: Which of those three things would you like to focus on first?

PLAYER: The bit about handling questions. That was the worst bit.

Options

Once the clearest possible understanding of the situation or topic has been reached, the discussion naturally turns to what can be done—to what it is possible for the player to do. I use 'possible' as in 'that's a possibility'—in the biggest, most creative sense, rather then in a narrow, restrictive one. In the **reality** phase, a clear understanding is gained, and it is from this understanding that the possibilities emerge.

The intention here is to draw out a list of all that is possible without judgment or evaluation:

> COACH: We've spoken about preparation, nervousness, and handling questions in some depth now. In looking to move forward, which of those would you like to pursue first?
> PLAYER: I still think there is most mileage in the 'handling questions' bit. If I can get that right, it will help with the nervousness issue, and the preparation bit should be easy to crack.
> COACH: Where we got to with handling questions, as I understood you, was that you felt that you had not always fully understood the question.
> PLAYER: Yes, and that was partly because I was thinking of my next slide.
> COACH: So what could you do differently?
> PLAYER: I could make sure that no questions were asked until the end of the session.
> COACH: What else?
> PLAYER: I could just stop myself from going to the next slide—maybe make eye contact. That would help.
> COACH: Anything else?
> PLAYER: Not sure. Well, if I haven't heard I could ask the questioner to repeat the question, or if I think I've heard but I'm not sure, I suppose I could check my understanding by repeating the question.
> COACH: What else can you think of?

Wrap-up

This is the final stage of the model, with lots of options on the table. What remains is to select the most appropriate and agree the next steps. It is often useful to check the player's commitment to the chosen course of action, and to see if any support is required. It is almost always useful to get the player to say exactly what their action plan is. If the player states the action plan, it ensures clarity and agreement—and, from the tone of voice, the coach can ascertain the level of commitment.

In this stage, the coach's intention is to gain commitment to action:

COACH: Of all the options that we have identified, which ones do you think you might action?
PLAYER: I can't remember them all.
COACH: I think I jotted down most of them. There are those options that came out of the discussion about the presentation, concerning preparation, nervousness, and handling questions. Then there were the options that came out of the second part of the discussion. Where do you want to start?
PLAYER: Let's start with the handling questions bit.
COACH: You came up with four options: keeping the questions to the end of the session, stopping and making eye contact, asking the questioner to repeat the question, and playing your understanding of the question back.
PLAYER: That's right. The only one I'm uncomfortable about is the first one: keeping questions till the end.
COACH: What is it that makes you uncomfortable?
PLAYER: Despite the fact that I am not very good at it—yet—I do want to keep the sessions as interactive as possible. So I think I'll skip that one. The others I can do.
COACH: Just so we are both sure, tell me specifically what you are going to do?
PLAYER: In the presentation to the board, when I hear a question I will stop thinking of what I have to do next and make eye contact with the questioner. If I don't hear the question fully, I will either ask the person to repeat it—or, if I've got the gist of it, I will check my understanding by playing it back.
COACH: OK. Now which part do you want to tackle next?

The GROW model: a summary

Let me see if I can make this even clearer with an analogy. It is not entirely watertight, but it works very well in as far as it goes. When the player begins to talk, it is most likely that their thoughts about the topic are unclear and jumbled up. It's a bit like a jigsaw puzzle, only in this case the pieces are in a bag, and there is no cover picture to act as a guide. As the player talks, the corner pieces and some of the edges are identified and put on the table. The scale and the nature of the topic thus become a little clearer. At this point, it is possible to set a goal (outcome), as both the coach and the player exactly know what they are discussing, even if not all the details are clear. Moving to the reality phase, the player is encouraged to put all the pieces of the jigsaw—or almost all of them—on the table.

As the conversation progresses, the player will notice that some of the pieces are face down and others are in the wrong place. As most of the pieces are turned face-up and shuffled into the right place, a picture or pattern emerges. At this point, the player is in all probability in self two; seeing the whole picture, he will find new insight or come to a solution or a possible option. From this point onward, the player can usually begin to make some choices about the next steps.

The GROW model is shown above as a circle because in the most straightforward sessions you move from topic to goal to reality to options to wrap-up and then maybe agree a time and a place for the next conversation. The arrows between the stages reflect the fact that not all sessions are straightforward, and that you may have to shuffle between the stages. For instance, in the wrap-up stage the player may identify a new option, or in the reality stage it may become clear that the goal is not appropriate. If this happens, simply return to the relevant part of the model. Do not get stuck in its linear nature—few players think in a strictly linear fashion, and it is your job to follow their interest.

The Model T

As I have said, the role of the coach is to encourage players to think, but not to think for them. You need to stay on *their* agenda and to follow *their* interest. This is not an easy thing to do at first, because your instinct will likely be to think about the issue and try to solve it. What I have noticed over the years is that when I suggest that an instinctive response will not help the player, many coaches in training are at a loss as to what to do instead.

This is where the Model T—so named because of the way it is presented diagrammatically—comes in. The Model T is a remarkably powerful technique for making progress in the GROW model. It suggests that you expand the conversation first, then focus on the detail.

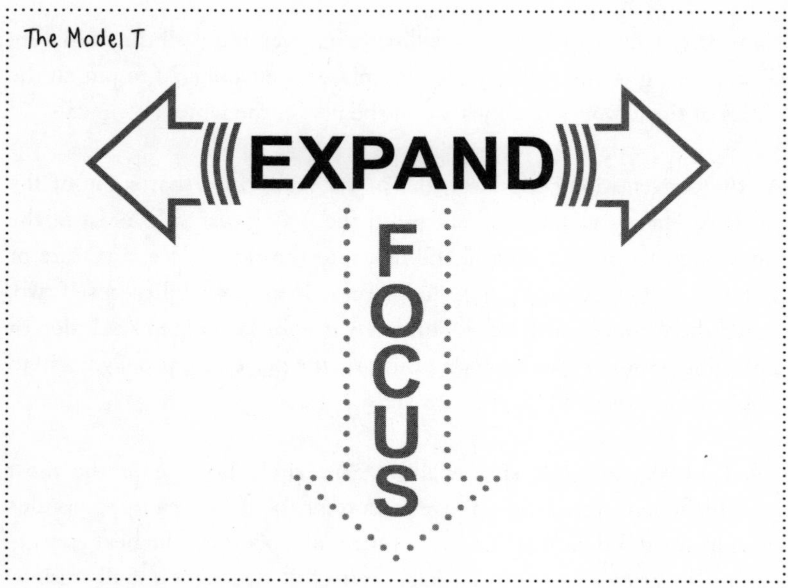

Imagine that you are in the options stage of the model. The conversation would go like this:

COACH: You've given me one option: to delegate the project to Jamie. What other options are there? *(Expanding)*
PLAYER: I could give it to Jamie but still supervise it myself.
COACH: Anything else? *(Expanding again)*
PLAYER: I could do it myself.
COACH: Anything else?
PLAYER: I can't think of anything.
COACH: OK. But let's see if there are any other options. Tell me what you would really like to do, regardless of consequences? *(Expanding again, and adding a little creativity.)*
PLAYER: Well, what I'd really like is not to do it at all. But ... that's not realistic. Having said that, I could delay it for a couple of weeks till I'm less busy.
COACH: So, four options then: hand it to Jamie completely; hand it to Jamie and you supervise; do it yourself; and delay it till later. Which of those is most interesting? *(Focusing and leaving choice and responsibility with the player.)*

The Model T has some inherent benefits. Often, in coaching, the temptation is to seek resolution as quickly as possible. There are many dangers in this, not least that the coach starts driving the agenda. A second danger is that, in an attempt to make progress, information that might be relevant is omitted. The Model T keeps the coach on the player's agenda, and because it suggest that you expand the conversation before going into detail, most if not all of the relevant information is picked up in the conversation.

The model should also be used in the topic or reality phases. If a player describes a particular aspect of an issue and the coach asks him to 'tell me some more about that' (focusing), there is the possibility that time will be invested in discussing something that is not entirely relevant to the overall issue. Far better is to ask if there is anything else (expanding) and then, having heard any other aspects of the issue, to focus on the aspect that appears to be most relevant.

It is the Model T and the notion of following interest that is that core of what I would have previously called a non-directive approach.

> COACH: So, you've told me that the project is behind, and that you're going to miss the next milestone, and you've also mentioned the poor performance of your team. Is there anything else? *(Summarizing, then expanding.)*
> PLAYER: We have an internal client, a sponsor from the board, who is also slowing things down.
> COACH: The project, the team, and the sponsor. Which is most interesting to discuss first? *(Focusing.)*
> PLAYER: Actually, we should really talk about the sponsor. When we started the conversation I thought it was really all about the poor performance of the team, but without a clear remit from our sponsor it is always going to be difficult to be successful.

In this snippet of conversation, you can see that if the coach had not 'expanded', a really important element of the issue might have been overlooked. The coach also used the word 'interesting' in the focusing question. Initially, this surprises people; they expect words like 'relevant' or 'important'. If the coach had used the word 'important' instead, there is a possibility that it might have generated interference and pushed the player into self one or a fixed mindset. The player might well become less relaxed as he tries to make the 'right' choice in a matter that the coach had indicated was 'important'. It's far better to follow interest where there is less danger of judgment. Interest allows room for intuition and feelings, among other things, and will almost always generate a richer conversation.

– CHAPTER 7 –

The skills of effective coaching

This short chapter is an introduction to the skills of effective coaching, and the purpose in writing it is twofold. Firstly, I want to bring together in one place all the skills that go to make up an effective coach so that the breadth and depth of the task of learning to coach can be appreciated. Secondly, I want to introduce a 'tool': the notion of intent that defines the use and application of each of the skills.

The chart below shows many and varied skills. The inclusion of some of the skills, such as listening and asking questions, is obvious, while the presence of some others, such as hypothesizing, may be less so. This chart is an attempt to bring together all the skills that make a coach effective, and as a consequence it includes skills that are not necessarily deployed within the coaching conversation. I know that some part of the value that I add in coaching comes from the thinking I do when I am walking the dog, or because I have taken time to interview the people with whom the person I am coaching works, and therefore have a good understanding of their organizational context, the key people, the culture, the strategy, and so on.

In the chart, I have grouped the various skills into skill sets, each defined by a common intent. The skill sets are shown in the left-hand column of the chart. I then show the outward manifestation—the specific skill—in the right-hand column. Some skills show up in more than one set. The middle column describes the intent.

The notion of intent

Let me explain what I mean by intent in relation to the skills of coaching,

Coaching skills and intents

SKILL SETS	INTENT	SPECIFIC SKILLS
Generating understanding/ raising awareness	To help the player understand themself / their situation more fully so that they can make better decisions	• Listening in order to understand • Repetition, paraphrasing and summarising • Using silence • Asking questions that follow interest • Asking questions to clarify • Grouping
Proposing	To make available to the player the coach's observations, knowledge, experience, intelligence, insight, intuition and wisdom	• Giving feedback • Making suggestions • Giving advice • Challenging • Evoking creativity and innovation • Giving instruction
Managing self	To ensure that the impact of the coach's needs and preconceptions on the player are minimised To maximise one's own performance as coach	• Self awareness • Boundary awareness • Transparency • Clarifying intent • Entering 'flow'/Self Two
Structuring	To ensure that the player achieves meaningful results from the coaching	• Following interest • Using the GROW model and the Model T • Setting goals
Building relationship	To create an environment in which the player feels safe and unjudged	• Generating understanding (as above) • Creating a contract
Understanding organisational context	To ensure that the coaching engagement meets the client's needs	• Generating understanding (as above) • Hypothesising/testing hypotheses

and how by understanding this you can learn to be more effective. Skills are the stuff of the 'outer game', as are behaviours and competencies. They can be described and measured, and you get a sense of what is to be done. But the notion of 'competencies'—so beloved by those who would reengineer our organizations (and who really wants to be merely competent, when genius is available?)—is insufficient to our task. This is because it gives you no idea of when or why to deploy the skill or behaviour or, critically, to what effect. I may know quite well that a particular style of question—an open question, say—is a useful tool, but if I deploy it indiscriminately I will not help the player.

If the skills are of the outer game, there is a corresponding inner game. Real effectiveness lies in understanding both the inner and outer components. In training coaches and managers, I frequently observe them practising coaching. When I notice that they have asked a question or made an intervention that does not seem to help the player I often ask: 'What was your intent?'

Intent is the inner game of finding the appropriate question. By intent, I mean the purpose or aim of the coach when deploying one or more of the skills. In coaching (and not *just* in coaching), understanding one's own intent at any moment is a key component in becoming more effective. When I ask novice coaches the intent question, I get many kinds of answers. Mostly they point to the coach's need to solve, to fix, to heal, to be right, or to be in control; the intentions seldom help the player become more aware or retain responsibility.

The following snippet of conversation between in a player in a workshop, a coach-in-training, and a programme leader, is typical of what often occurs.

PLAYER: As I see it, there are two things I can do. I can ask my manager to review the decision, or I can do what I think is best and hope he doesn't find out.
COACH: Have you thought of involving the rest of the team?
PROGRAMME LEADER: What is your intent with this question?
COACH: Well, the two options are a bit risky, and I think he needs to find another approach.
PROGRAMME LEADER: So there are two parts to this: that you think it's risky, and that you think he needs another approach. So what specifically is your intent?
COACH: I guess I was trying to steer him toward what I think he should do.
PROGRAMME LEADER: What might be a more appropriate intent?
COACH: Well ... first to help him assess the possible risks in the approaches he's identified, and then, if the risks are great, to think through other options.
PROGRAMME LEADER: So what's the question for the player?
COACH: I could ask him what might happen if he pursued either of the approaches he identified.

In being clear about intent, the coach tends to ask more effective questions. But understanding one's intent gives you more than that: it also speaks directly to self two, and thus enables questions to flow with little or no effort, and with great accuracy. And that's so much more fun.

– CHAPTER 8 –

Generating understanding and raising awareness

This chapter concerns one of the skill sets shown in the chart in the previous chapter. These skills are at the core of effective coaching, and not being proficient in them is simply not an option for a coach.

In this skill set, the intent is to help the player understand himself and his situation more fully, so that he can make better decisions than he would have done anyway. Notice that I have not said the *right* decision. When I first came upon *The Inner Game of Tennis*, I was very excited and gave it to my mother to read. She had been a successful tennis player, and I wanted her to understand my excitement. She took the book away and read it. On returning it to me, she said: 'I did not understand a word of it, but if it makes a difference to you, that is all that matters.'

I will not accuse my mother of being disingenuous, but clearly she had understood something: it may not be the 'right' thing or decision from a given perspective, but if it enables the player to move forward and learn—and does not damage him or the interests of the organization—then it is far better to let the player pursue it. The primary function of the coach is to understand. Not to solve, fix, heal, make better, or be wise; to understand. The magic is that it is in that moment of understanding that the player understands for himself, becomes more aware, and is then in a position to make better decisions and choices than he would have done previously.

In this way, coaching is profoundly simple, and simply profound. But most of us struggle to get above our own agenda, and instead want to be seen to be making a difference.

The following are the specific skills of generating understanding/raising awareness:

- Listening to understand
- Repetition, paraphrasing, summarizing
- Grouping
- Silence
- Asking questions that follow interest
- Asking questions to clarify.

In the following sections I describe each of the specific skills in some depth.

Listening to understand

In this relationship between you and me, the closest we can get to the experience of listening is your attending to the words on the page. A blank page would be the closest that I could get to silence within the confines of a book. As you look at this blank page, it is my guess that your experience is not of blankness but rather of all the ideas that you could read into the page.

'Is this a mistake?'
'What a waste of paper!'
'Have I missed something?'

In effect, you fill the page with your own thoughts.

As another example, next time you are in a position where someone else is speaking, take the opportunity to notice your own listening. If you are like the rest of us, the quality of it will be inconsistent, and probably dependent on your level of interest in what is being said. In some moments your attention will be completely with the speaker; in others it will drift. Some particular point may hold your attention, and you begin to relate to some other matter … and all of a sudden you are away with the fairies. Perhaps the speaker is a little boring, or maybe he doesn't express himself well. Your own judgments creep in, followed, in short order, by your expectations, opinions, and assumptions.

Even as you read this page, your thoughts might spin off in some flight of fantasy, or something in the environment will distract you. Listening is a fundamental skill, and paying attention should be easy. Sometimes, in a workshop, I will give the participants a simple listening exercise. When the exercise is over, I will ask them what got in the way of their listening—what were the interferences?—and will note down their responses. Here is a typical list:

- 'Other people talking.'
- 'What I thought they were going to say.'
- 'What I thought they should say.'
- 'They were boring.'
- 'I had already worked out what they should do.'
- 'I had thought of what they were saying already.'
- 'What I was thinking was more interesting.'
- 'I was thinking of the next question.'
- 'I was thinking of my response.'
- 'What's for dinner?'
- 'Why is he wearing that tie?'

That little voice in your head works overtime, and it is difficult to stop it. Mostly this noise comes directly from self one, and has no earthly use. There is so much going on in our own minds that to make sufficient space for another is difficult. At this point in the workshop, some participants get upset. They value their own thoughts and ideas; they are entertained by their assumptions and revel in their judgments. This is fine, of course, as long as they do not try to coach someone, or pretend that they are listening.

Forgive me for repeating myself. In coaching, the purpose of listening is to understand, because that in turn generates understanding and awareness in the player. Many of us listen not with the intention to understand but with the intention to respond: we are just waiting for the speaker to take a breath so that we can get to speak or—almost as bad—using the time when the other is speaking to think up the next question or a suitable response.

In doing some work with an international consultancy some years ago, where the consultants were renowned for their intelligence, a senior partner informed me: 'People around here don't listen, they reload!' But there is another way. Imagine a spring-loaded stack of plates such as you might find in a canteen. As you take the top plate, the next one is pushed up. Each plate represents an idea or notion that rises into the consciousness of the player. As a thought enters the consciousness and is passed on to a listener, the space for the next thought is created. And that one is passed on, followed by the next one. Somewhere down in the player's stack of plates—in their mind—is his solution, his creative idea, his insight. If someone is willing to listen, the player may get to that plate—that thought. And because the thought is uniquely his own, he will nurture it, develop it, and put it to some creative use.

On the other hand, if the coach takes the first few plates, assumes that he now understands, and then gives the player back the plates plus a few more of his own—his own good ideas, or his way forward—then no real learning has occurred, and the player does not own the outcome. And if the coach is also the manager, not only does this mean the solution, idea, or insight further down the stack, it also means that in order to get to it, the player has to challenge the manager's authority. Another good idea lost, another breakthrough unheard—and a demotivated employee.

There are a number of things you can do to improve your listening. The first is simple, but not necessarily easy. Start noticing when you are not listening, and gently bring your attention back to the speaker. This has one major flaw as a tactic, in that the only time you become aware that you have 'gone away with your thoughts' is when you return, or when the speaker gives you some feedback—which may be too late. If this does happen, the only response with any integrity is to own up. The speaker is unlikely to be surprised; he or she will have noticed, probably before you did.

The second thing is a discipline called 'managing your communication cycles'. I find this particularly useful when demonstrating coaching in public. The potential for distraction is so great, and nerves so jangled, that I need something quite overt to keep me focused.

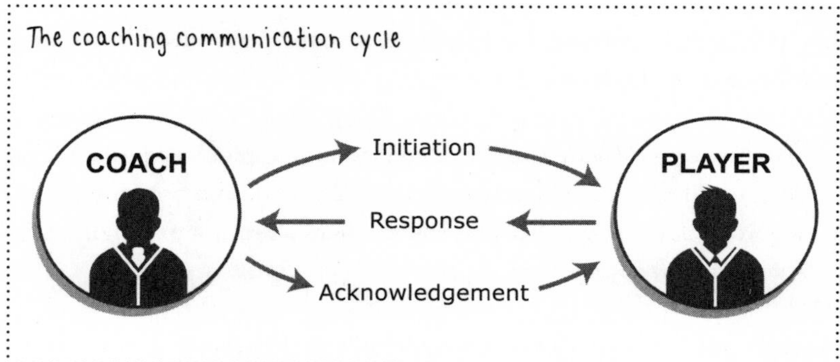

The **communication cycle** shown below is used to help you manage conversations in which there is a need for a high order of understanding. You do not need to do this for every conversation; indeed, if you did you would exhaust yourself and those around you.

A prerequisite for communication is a minimum of two people—in this case, a coach and a player. The first part of the cycle is called **initiation**: the coach asks a question or issues an instruction to the player. The second part is called the **response**, the player having understood the initiation answers. The answer must be congruent with the initiation.

> COACH: Tell me how you got on with your action plan from our last session. *(Initiation)*
> PLAYER: I had a truly miserable week. One of my clients pulled out of a deal at the last minute and … *(Incongruent response)*
> COACH: I'm sorry, we can return to that if you want, but tell me: how did the action plan go?
> PLAYER: Oh, the action plan: I got most of it done, I'd say 90%. I couldn't complete writing up my career vision because I ran out of time. Not bad, considering the difficulties. *(Congruent response)*

The cycle is not complete here, however. The cycle is only complete when the player knows that he has been understood. So the final part is called acknowledgment. At the start of a session, particularly with a new client, the acknowledgment will take the form of a full summary or paraphrasing of what has been said. This is because the coach needs to be absolutely certain that he has understood, and also because the player needs reassuring that he has been understood.

> COACH: Let me check that I've understood. Despite some difficulties, you got 90% of the action plan done. The bit you did not quite finish was your career vision, because you ran out of time. Is that right? *(Acknowledgment)*

As the session progresses and trust develops in the relationship, the need to summarize or paraphrase diminishes. You will still need to manage your communication cycles, but for now, 'I understand' or a grunt or a nod of the head signals the acknowledgment.

Another way to signal that you have understood is to ask a further question congruent with the response.

> COACH: Tell me about the difficulties. (Congruent question/initiation)

The cycle completes, and a new one starts. This may seem like a tedious process to engage in, and I would not recommend you use it while discussing the weather with your neighbour as it will drive both of you mad and rapidly diminish the number of friends and acquaintances you have. Only use it when there is a need for high-quality communication, such as in coaching.

As with the GROW model, I would like you to know that for the most part it happens quite naturally, and typically goes unnoticed by the player. His experience is of being completely understood, probably for the first time. This builds trust in the relationship and raises awareness, but it also does one other thing. It is also a bit like using the 'Save' command on your computer: all the important information is now safely stored (understood), and the player can feel free to move on to the next point. It can thus create a flow in the conversation not unlike the earlier image of the stack of plates.

From my own experience, I know that when engaging with a new client, with a difficult issue, it is the discipline of managing the communication cycles that has generated real understanding and been the foundation of a successful conversation.

Repeating, Summarizing, and Paraphrasing

The most powerful aspects of generating understanding and raising awareness are repetition, summarizing, and paraphrasing. And let me remind you again of the intent: to help the player understand himself and his situation more fully, so that he can make better decisions than he would have done before. In using these skills, something special can happen. As the coach repeats what has been said, summarizes, or paraphrases, the player often has a new insight or idea. I can only guess as to why that might happen. I think it is that, as the player hears the issue played back, it is possible to get a little distance (a concept explored later in this chapter) from the issue; no longer so attached, he is able to see it differently, and to have new thoughts on the matter. You might have noticed that it is always easier to solve someone else's problem than your own—that is, when there really is distance.

Repetition or repeating verbatim gives a clear signal to the player that you have at least heard the words. But a tape recorder can do that too. What it does not do is signal that you have fully understood. But it has its place in coaching when a particular set of words—or a single word—has significance for the player. This is even more important when there is an emotional undertone. That you have picked up on that significance is a demonstration that you have understood.

> COACH: If I remember correctly, earlier in the conversation you said that the team's decision 'didn't just upset me but destroyed my self-confidence'.
> PLAYER: Exactly, and it is both of those things. They are both important to sort out.

Summarizing is to present in shortened form or to extract the essence and is another demonstration that you have understood. **Paraphrasing** differs in that you knowingly choose to substitute your own words (or word) for the player's. You might do this to check your own understanding, or because you believe that the new word or words are in fact a better expression of what the player means. It is a great way of checking that you have actually understood what the player has said.

In coaching, these tools are best used to check understanding, for example after the player has made a number of points, or at the end of a stage of the GROW model. Another effective way to use them is to turn them around and have the player summarize or paraphrase. It can generate great clarity of what is truly important for the player. It is also a good trick if you have lost the thread and either do not have the courage to own up or deem it inappropriate: 'There was a lot there. Could you summarize it for me?'

Grouping

Grouping (or chunking) is the ability to identify the principal themes, elements, or chunks of a conversation, and to play these back to the player. Doing so typically has the effect of increasing understanding, and that is indeed the intent. Sometimes, the player is confronted with a problem of magnitude and complexity. It occurs to them as an undifferentiated mess—pea soup. If the coach can identify the various elements, it makes understanding easier: 'So far you've mentioned stock, cream, herbs—but you did not say which herbs—and, of course, peas.'

In the coaching conversation in chapter 1, Henry had been speaking for quite some time before Melanie summarizes:

> 'Then, if I have understood, there are three parts to this: the ability of the project team, a shift in the financial parameters, and the differing needs of our two friends, Steve and Jeremy.'
>
> 'That's right. Although, on the third point, it's as much about the pressure they put on me as it is about their "needs", as you put it.'
>
> 'OK. So four things then, including the pressure they are putting on you. Which would be most interesting to talk about first?'

At its most complex, grouping involves the ability to differentiate, and to see that things belong to the same set. To continue the culinary metaphor, 'You have mentioned the vegetables and the fruit. In the vegetable category you have cabbages and carrots, and in the fruit category you have oranges, apples, and pears.'

Silence

Novice coaches are often afraid of silences in their coaching conversations, and will jump in with another question to avoid it. A lot of valuable reflection can be lost when this happens. Silence is truly golden in coaching. Typically it means that the player is busy thinking or processing something for himself. When he is ready, he will tell you. There is, of course, another kind of silence, which occurs when the player does not know what he is supposed to be doing, in which case it is down to the coach to move the session on. It is usually pretty easy to tell when someone is thinking something through (lots of eye movement, concentration) and when they're not (vacant look, distraction), so look for the physical signals.

Asking questions that follow interest

Another way of deepening understanding, and thereby raising awareness, is to ask questions.

We have looked at asking questions that follow interest elsewhere in this book already, so there is no need to repeat the information here. But to reinforce the notion of intent, I will suggest that this skill is a way of enabling the player to move forward as a function of his or her own thinking and choices. It is non-directive coaching at its best. In following interest, the player becomes very focused, thus removing interference and in turn allowing full access to his intelligence, imagination, and intuition.

There is another way to describe this that seems to be helpful. I call it floodlight and spotlight. **Floodlight** comes first, shedding light on the whole territory and into every nook and cranny. Then comes the **spotlight**, which brings light to a specific aspect—chosen, most often, by the player, following interest. (Of course, the player can direct the player's attention, and I will address that later in this chapter, under 'Proposing'.)

My own coach, Cliff Kimber, will frequently ask me: 'What do you need to think clearly about?' It's great question.

Questions that clarify

The 'W' questions—what, who, where, and when—are all useful in raising awareness. And then an 'H' question: how, or how much. Notice that I have not included why. I'll come back to that shortly.

What — or, better still, 'what specifically is that?'— is useful when someone uses a word that you have not come across before.

PLAYER: And so, without telling anyone, they removed all the codals.
COACH: What specifically is a codal?
(I cannot take this example any further because in order to make the point, I had to find a noun that no one would know. So I had to make one up.)

In most meetings, it would not be the end of the world if you did not understand a particular word. You would merely wait for the break and ask a trusted colleague. In a coaching session, where what drives the session is understanding, you simply cannot afford to miss the meaning. 'What' is also useful when a player uses a word that you do recognize:

PLAYER: In this company I get absolutely no acknowledgment.
COACH: What do you mean by acknowledgment?
PLAYER: A little bit of praise now and again.

You see, everyone else thought that the salary was acknowledgment enough.

Who is useful in two ways. The first way to use it is when someone uses a pronoun (he, she, they, it) but you are not sure who is being referred to. (Just don't ask all the questions at once.)

PLAYER: He said to her that they should all do it together.
COACH: Let me just check that. Who specifically said it? To whom? Who specifically are they? And what is it that they should do?

The second way is to get a complete list of all the characters that might have an impact on the topic of the coaching conversation. 'Who else is involved? Who are the other members of the team?'

Where and **when** give specific location in time and place:

> PLAYER: I am completely stuck with this report.
> COACH: Where exactly in the report are you stuck?
> PLAYER: Well, the main part of it is fine, I'm just having difficulty in drawing out the conclusions for the summary.

In this example, a worry gets identified as something very specific, and the coaching can proceed.

> PLAYER: I'll talk to Paul soon.
> COACH: When exactly?
> PLAYER: Tomorrow, before 12.

In this example, a loose commitment that could easily be misunderstood—soon could mean a few minutes or a few weeks—quickly becomes a firm agreement.

How is a useful question. It is always used in connection with verbs—'doing' words. It gets to high-quality information very quickly. I learnt this in a somewhat painful manner, as the following anecdote shows.

Charles was my early mentor. We travelled around the UK together for a couple of years, running coaching workshops. This was my apprenticeship. There was, however, a problem associated with all this travel. When I left home to go to a workshop, I would upset the balance and dynamics at home, which was not entirely popular. (I would also like to think that I was missed.) When I was away, another routine was established, so my return upset this in turn, making me doubly unpopular. And on my return, I was typically exhausted and incapable of normal human interaction. So I asked Charles—he being older and wiser than me—if there was anything I could do to overcome this problem.

Charles looked at me and said: 'Sinead and I, we rebop.'

'What specifically is that?' I asked.
Charles was just getting on a train and responded through the open window in the door. 'It's a semi-erotic, semi-therapeutic activity for two consenting adults.'

By the time I realised that I was really none the wiser, it was too late; the train had pulled out of the station. I had made a fundamental mistake: I had asked the **what** question (for nouns) when I should have asked a **how** question.

The next time I met up with Charles, I had worked it out. 'Charles,' I asked, 'how do you do that, rebop?'

Charles was in a taciturn mood, however, and asked me if I was a Catholic. I was not, but I had been brought up as one. Given that, and the fact that I was not yet married to my now-wife, Jo, Charles said he could not, in all conscience, tell me!

As I have said, the 'what' question refers to nouns, the 'how' to verbs. Ask the right question and you get high-quality information, thus contributing to understanding. For example:

> PLAYER: I need to learn how to manage my team better.
> COACH: How do you learn?
> PLAYER: I'm not sure. I like to watch others and read a bit. And then I like to give it a go.

The player has pretty much defined an action plan in response to one simple question.

How much adds clarity and raises awareness when matters of quantity, size, or scale are under discussion.

> PLAYER: We are almost certainly going to fall short of the budgeted target for sales.

COACH: By how much?

A response such as

PLAYER: Only by 3%.

is very different from

PLAYER: I guess it could be as much as $5,000,000.

Depending on the scale of the issue, the coaching will follow very different paths.

There is another version of the 'how much' question that has a very similar intent: to raise awareness.

PLAYER: I am really concerned about the new strategy Bob presented yesterday.
COACH: How concerned, on a scale of one to ten?
PLAYER: That's a good question. Actually only about three or four.
COACH: So do we need to discuss it now?
PLAYER: No, it's more important that we talk through the conference next week.

If the response to the 'how much' question had been eight, then there is no doubt the coach and player would have talked about Bob's new strategy.

I excluded **why** from my list of questions that clarify. More often than not, 'why' elicits reasons, justifications, and excuses—none of which is useful in raising awareness. There is also the possibility of pushing the player into self one. 'Why?' does not create distance. It is also a pretty sloppy question. It can mean so many things, from 'What is your purpose?' to 'What is your reason?' to blame, as in 'But why?'

Instead, you should ask a more specific question:

'What is your purpose in that?'
'What were the reasons behind that decision?'
'What is it that makes that important for you?'

Some other questions

I want to include some further types of question for which I could find no obvious category but which can be very effective. One of the mistaken impressions that people get in being introduced to the notion of what has been termed non-directive coaching is that the coach has to be gentle with the player that the coach cannot get tough. Tying players down to specifics and getting them to commit are parts of the toolkit. These are aspects of the skill of 'challenging' which I address in chapter 9:

1. Get specific.

PLAYER: Well, that has been a useful conversation. I'll try a couple of the things we discussed over the next few weeks.
COACH: Great. Tell me, what specifically you are going to do? And by when?

2. Commit.

PLAYER: I think I might have a go at giving Paul some feedback.
COACH: You sound a little unsure. What are you actually going to do?

Lastly, before we move on I would like to remind you of the description of the ball-catching demonstration in chapter 2. Peter's natural ability to catch manifested when he was focused—when there was no interference. It's the same for you as a coach. If you are completely focused and interested in your player's learning, your natural instinct to coach—self two—will manifest, and you will ask an appropriate question.

I am aware that this could sound like completely unscientific, pop-psychology nonsense. Mammals have developed a capacity called limbic resonance. If I remember my physics classes properly, when an object that is vibrating at a particular frequency is put in closer proximity to an object of similar material and size, the second object will begin to vibrate at the same frequency. Limbic resonance allows two mammals to become aware of each other's internal state. It is this resonance that makes 'non-directive' coaching impossible—the human being cannot 'not communicate'.

It is through this mechanism that a significant amount of the human being's essential learning occurs, in proximity with the parent. This capacity does not desert us as adults, and it enables us to ask the next question, particularly when we are in self two. Once the coach has practised sufficiently to know the basics to the point that they have become unconscious acts, our intuitions and instincts become valuable.

In any case, it does not particularly matter if you make a mistake. Coaching is not an exam, and you do not get only one chance. If a question does not work, ask another. When you are in a good relationship, it does not matter. There is only one mistake you can make in coaching, and that is to irreparably damage the relationship.

Finally in this section on questions, please do not worry about the 'right' question to ask. Do not get stuck in your doubts or the models, but simply get interested: if you're stuck, your attention is with you and not with the player. One of the best questions I was ever asked while being coached went like this:

> 'I don't know what the next question is. Do you?
> And of course I did.

Postscript

The issue of distance, referred to a little earlier in this chapter, is important in coaching. If a player is caught up in a difficult or emotional topic there is no distance. He really is the problem.

I remember sitting on the top deck of a London bus one day as it travelled into the West End in heavy traffic. As the bus approached a junction, I could see, before it actually happened, that we were heading for a complete logjam. Four cars at the junction had managed to get into positions from which none could easily move.

From the top of the bus, it was easy to see the solution. If the blue car just pulled back a few feet, that would allow the red car …

For the driver of the blue car, however, it is a different matter. He gets angry and frustrated: 'Just what I need when I'm late. Where did that @*^! > in the red car come from? Shouldn't be allowed on the road …' He has become the problem. If he could only see it—the logjam, and himself, from the top of the bus—he might also see the solution.

It is the job of the effective coach to get the player—the driver, in this analogy—out of the jam and up onto the top of the bus, to get some distance. I used the jigsaw analogy in the description of the GROW model. This is the same thing—and this is what I mean by raising awareness. The process of talking to the coach and then of reflecting back through either summarizing or the gentle raising of an eyebrow—of simply being understood—can create that distance.

The skills described in this chapter are all situated at the non-directive end of the range of coaching approaches. The intent that I ascribed to this skill set is to help the player understand himself and his situation more fully so that he can make better decisions. In the next chapter, we slide a little to the left of the range, toward the more directive skills—but with caution.

– CHAPTER 9 –

Proposing

I approach this chapter with the tiniest degree of trepidation. My concern is that, in devoting a whole chapter to the skills at the directive end of the range of coaching approaches, I might be seen to be giving equal weight to these skills. This is not what I intend to communicate.

In any coaching conversation, I spend approximately 90% of my time following interest or, to use my previous term, at the non-directive end of the range, because that is what is most effective. There are occasions in coaching—and always fewer than you think—where the coach has something of value to add. This set of skills, which I call 'proposing', is perhaps the most difficult skill set to apply effectively because of the inherent dangers of removing responsibility and choice from the player. The paradox is that the directive approach is the traditional model, and is where we typically begin. Toward the end of this chapter, I have included a short section on 'transparency', to help overcome this difficulty, and also put forward four tests for the coach to apply when about to propose.

Proposing requires a different skill set from generating understanding or raising awareness as it covers the skills used when the coach chooses to make an input rather than drawing information from the player. In The *Chambers Dictionary*, the definition of the word 'propose' is given as 'to put forward or exhibit, to bring to one's own or another person's attention'. The latter part of the definition is particularly appropriate, as it acknowledges that while the coach may, for example, make a suggestion, the player does not have to include it in his thinking or act on it. To propose is not to impose.

Let me remind you of the intent in proposing. It is to make available to the player the coach's observations, knowledge, experience, intelligence, insight, intuition, and wisdom. The result, however, is ultimately the same as for generating understanding and raising awareness: to help the player understand himself and his situation more fully so that he can make better decisions than he would have done otherwise.

The following are the specific skills of proposing, which I describe in detail in this chapter:

- Giving feedback
- Making suggestions
- Giving advice
- Instructing
- Challenging
- Evoking creativity
- Transparency.

Giving feedback

Unfortunately, giving and receiving feedback is optional. I know it could not be any other way, but you have only to ask two questions of people in most organizations to be very clear that there is not a whole lot of it happening.

The first question is this: 'Have you given any feedback recently?' The answer is almost always yes. Then you ask: 'Have you received any feedback recently?' and the answer is invariably no.

If you ask these questions across an organization, you can form a number of hypotheses, one of which is that there will be an incredibly sorted person—someone you have missed because he is locked up in the basement—getting all the feedback. Another is that not much feedback is being given. A third and more generous conclusion is that people think they are giving feedback when in fact they are merely alluding to something, or dropping hints. Whichever is the case, the vast majority of us do not receive sufficient feedback.

This is an important issue. The body–mind is a cybernetic system. That is to say, it requires feedback from its environment in order to function properly. Another example of a cybernetic system is a guided missile—a bit out of place in this book, perhaps, especially since resorting to violence does rather fall off the directive end of the range of coaching approaches, but it makes the point. A guided missile requires feedback to know whether it is on target or not.

A sensory deprivation chamber, or floatation tank, is a place where the body–mind gets virtually no feedback, and it is useful to look at what happens if someone is left in such a place for too long. A floatation tank is a bit like a bath, only bigger, usually about seven or eight feet square. It is filled to a depth of about 18 inches with a high-density saline solution at body temperature. It is totally enclosed. No light gets in, and no sound. You cannot feel much because you are floating, and you do not notice the water because it is at exactly the same temperature as your skin. In short, your senses are deprived of all or almost all stimulation. It is, after all, a sensory deprivation chamber.

An hour spent in a floatation tank has the effect of seven hours' sleep and is a powerful rejuvenating process. It can also put the mind in an extremely receptive state. Many people have solved nagging or serious problems or had creative ideas in a floatation tank. Some sportspeople use them in conjunction with video. In this receptive state, they see images of themselves performing perfectly, and thus train the muscle memory to repeat perfect performances. All very good, as long as you do not mind smelling faintly of Epsom salts for a week.

If you stay in the floatation tank for too long, however, you begin to hallucinate—you make it up. After a while, you go mad. There are lots of people walking around organizations who are hallucinating; many of them are senior executives to whom nobody feels able to tell the truth.

The consequence of not receiving feedback is that we make it up ourselves. You know that report that someone left on your desk last week, the one that you have not had time to read? Let me tell you now that they have already made up what happened: it was not good enough. And what can follow from 'it was not good enough' is often 'I am not good enough'. Let me say it again: when people do not know what the reality is, they make it up.

In workshops, it can be useful to ask people what stops them from giving feedback. A typical list of responses includes some of these ideas:

- 'It's not part of my job.'
- 'If they can't do the job they should not be here.'
- 'It's not in the culture.'
- 'I don't have time.'
- 'I don't have enough information.'
- 'Who am I to judge another?'
- 'I don't want to discourage them.'
- 'I don't want to hurt them.'

When pushed, most will acknowledge that not giving feedback comes down to that last answer: 'I don't want to hurt them.' Underneath it is another issue that I think it's worth being really clear about, and it is this: 'If I hurt you, you will not like me any more.' It's an understandable—but hardly noble—reason for withholding feedback.

Imagine this scenario: a chair, and behind it, about 15 feet away, a waste-paper basket. In the chair sits an unsuspecting volunteer. His task, the coach informs him, is to throw a ball over his head so that it lands in the basket. It must go straight in and not bounce. And no looking. The coach's job is to give the volunteer feedback.

The player throws a ball.

> COACH: You missed.
> PLAYER: Really?
> COACH: Have another go.

Another attempt.

COACH: You missed again.
PLAYER: By how much?
COACH: Listen, sunshine, I'm in a hurry. Get on with it.

Another attempt.

COACH: That was even worse.
PLAYER: What do you want me to do?
COACH: Just get the ball in the basket. I suppose it's worth another try.

Eventually, in exasperation, the player throws the ball at the coach. This conversation is noticeable for:

- The judgmental attitude of the coach
- The coach's lack of belief in the player's ability
- The coach making no attempt to create a relationship
- No usable data from the coach.

What is most worrying is that I occasionally demonstrate this conversation in workshops, and some participants start laughing. They can identify with the style only too well.

Now, the coach has learnt his lesson, and he tries again.

COACH: Thanks for volunteering. It's David, isn't it?
DAVID: Yes.
COACH: The exercise remains the same, and I'm wondering what you would like me to do to help.
DAVID: I'd like some real feedback.
COACH: And what exactly would you like from me?
DAVID: I'd like to know how far the ball was from the basket.
COACH: OK. And anything else?
DAVID: I guess you could tell me if it landed in front or behind the basket, and on which side.
COACH: OK. In front or behind and the side. How should I tell you how far away?

DAVID: What do you mean?
COACH: Feet? Feet and inches? Meters? That sort of thing.
DAVID: Oh no, I'm no good with distances. Just show me with your hands.
COACH: Ready to try?
DAVID: Yes. *(David throws.)*
COACH: The ball landed in front of the bucket, about this much *(he shows him with his hands)* and about the same distance to the left.

Within minutes, David will throw a ball in the basket. This conversation is noticeable for:

- A non-judgmental approach—just the data
- High-quality data
- Feedback in the form the player wanted it
- A stronger relationship
- The coach's belief in the player's potential (you'll have to take my word for it).

Before we go any further, I want to put something to bed. There is no such thing as negative feedback, and there is no such thing as positive feedback. There is just feedback—data. What happens is that people attach a judgment to the data to suit their purpose in that moment. That purpose is usually 'to be right'. And then the receiver responds to the judgment and not to the data. 'The boss is angry, so I won't do that again' is not a great way of getting to a good decision. The role of the coach is to give the data as cleanly as possible, so that the player can receive it, assess it, and make their own decision as to how to proceed.

That said, in giving feedback it is nigh impossible to communicate only the data. The receiver will also get some sense of your intent and the emotional charge that you carry. We must distinguish carefully between these three aspects of feedback:

DATA: This needs to be of the highest quality you can identify—the more specific the better. It also needs to be something that you have observed. Second-hand information frustrates people, because they cannot effectively challenge it. Examples help. Keep it free from judgment and interpretation.

INTENT: You must be really clear about your intent in giving the feedback. If it is to prove yourself right or to get one up on the receiver, it will not work. The only intent that has integrity is to raise awareness.

EMOTIONAL CHARGE: Are you angry, disappointed, elated? Whatever your emotions are, they will be communicated to some degree. You simply cannot help it. It is often useful to acknowledge this explicitly, so that you can manage yourself better.

Giving feedback in everyday work life

There is a useful three-step process to remember for giving feedback in the course of everyday work life:

- Contract
- Data
- Action.

Contract refers to the agreement you make with the person to whom you wish to give feedback. Ideally, the contract includes an **offer** and **clarity of intent**.

COACH: I have some feedback for you. Do you want it?

Usually, the answer is yes. If it is no, it might be appropriate to check the reason behind the rejection of the offer:

COACH: I appreciate that you don't want my feedback. May I ask why?
PLAYER: I'm really busy right now. Could we speak later?

Or:

> PLAYER: This is not a good place; it's too public. Can we use your office?

If the coach is also the manager, and the offer of feedback has been turned down and it is a critical, management issue, the line manager might have to insist on giving the feedback. 'I appreciate that you are not interested in my feedback, but it is my view that your approach to these meetings is jeopardizing the whole project. So I have a responsibility to give you the feedback. Do you want to have it now or later?'

The second element, clarity of intent, has already been demonstrated in the previous example. Another example is this: 'I want to make sure you are successful in running these meetings.'

As mentioned above, **data** should be of the highest quality possible, observed and owned by you, without judgment or interpretation. If it is a weighty matter, you might ask the player to self-assess: 'How do you see it?'

Subsets of the data step are situation, behaviour, and impact. 'In this afternoon's meeting about the Odyssey Project, when you questioned Jack (*situation*) I thought you were a little abrupt with him (*behaviour*). He seemed to me to be upset and demotivated as a result (*impact*).'

The feedback will almost certainly be ineffectual if there is no clarity or agreement about the **action** the player will do next. If it is a complex issue, the player may require further coaching, though you should not assume that you will be the coach. A simple question will often be sufficient, however: 'How might you help Jack get motivated again?' More generic examples include: 'How could you approach this kind of situation in the future?' and 'How, specifically, will you take this forward from here?'

Giving feedback in a coaching session

Many of the guidelines suggested above hold true for giving feedback in a coaching session. It is still important that the coach does not make an assumption that the player will welcome the feedback. If the session has been run in a non-directive fashion but then, suddenly and uninvited, the coach comes out with some feedback, it can be very disruptive to the session, and can damage the relationship. Without that relationship, there can be no coaching. The key is to offer the feedback, signalling clearly that this is a change of style, and then, once the feedback has been delivered, to move back into the non-directive mode:

> 'I've got some feedback for you. Do you want it?'
> 'What I have noticed is …'
> 'How does that fit in with what you've been saying?'
> 'Is that worth considering?'

I have occasionally had a player say no when I have offered to give feedback. When this happens, it is almost always because the player is busy thinking through another part of the issue and does not want to interrupt that process. When he is ready, I give the feedback. If he does not want it—which would be quite strange—I do not give it. If a pattern emerges in terms of a player continually refusing feedback, the coach might instead give feedback on the repeated refusals.

Making suggestions

In the context of coaching, suggestions are ideas that I believe to be appropriate to your situation. They arise in my mind as a function of my experience, my intelligence, my intuition, or my imagination. They are occasionally valid and occasionally acceptable to the player. As with feedback, the only issue is whether I can present them to the player in such a way as to give the player a genuine choice as to whether to accept them or not. The issue of choice can be influenced by a number of factors: my power in the relationship, my ability to influence, the player's desire to be influenced or to not have to take responsibility. There is a complexity here that no amount of written words can completely resolve, so let us return to what you can do. The guidelines are not dissimilar to those for offering feedback:

- Always present your suggestions as an offer: 'I've got a suggestion. Would you like to hear it?'
- When the suggestion has been heard, return to the non-directive ap-

proach: 'Does that work for you?' or 'We've identified a number of suggestions—w, x, y, and the one I threw in, z. Which of those is the most interesting?'

Giving advice

I have some problems with offering advice in a coaching session. It seems to me that offering advice suggests that the player and the coach do not see the situation from the same place. Advice suggests that the coach has not really been helpful in taking the player through the reality stage of the GROW model. When I give advice, I am making a stand for what I believe in, which means that I have probably stopped attending to the player's learning. So I tend not to give it.

I am, of course, presenting a rather narrow interpretation of advice. If you find yourself in the position of giving advice, the guidelines are the same as for any time you move from a non-directive mode. Make an offer, and if the advice is wanted, give it. Once it has been heard, return to the non-directive mode so that the player is left with choice.

Instructing

Giving instructions is sometimes appropriate in coaching sessions. What it implies is that there is a technique or approach that the coach knows, and that the player could not work out for himself, or that it would take more time for the player to work out himself than is available. As a tennis coach, I knew quite a bit about how to play tennis—the proper technique and way of doing things. Mostly, it just got in the way of the player's learning. These are some of the times, however, when instructions might be appropriate:

- When the player is tired
- When there is significant time pressure
- When the player is upset or panicking
- When the technique is complex (and known to the coach).

If you must give instructions, get permission to do so first, and then return to the non-directive mode straightaway. In my experience, in 90% of the times I have resorted to giving instructions it is because I, as the coach, have lost my way in the session, lost interest, or just become too tired.

The reality, of course, is that you can tell anyone to do anything. They just might not do it. Some people may sometimes do what you say, but that is because either they have surrendered their authority to you or they are unwilling to challenge your right to instruct, in which case we could not call it a coaching session. Very occasionally, I have told people what to do in a coaching session, but always with explicit permission. As far as I can remember, it is always when the player is so overwhelmed that he needs another to take control for a short while. That is OK, as long as it does not then result in the player becoming dependent on the coach.

Challenging

I have put this specific skill in the proposing section, although it could just as well sit in the section on generating understanding and raising awareness, for although challenging arises from the coach's understanding, its function is to raise awareness. True challenge comes from a belief in potential.

I remember coaching a senior manager in a large UK-based retail organization. Mike was given a project to restructure a major division of the organization, which would lead to some redundancies, but there were no clear objectives behind the project. When I asked how he could identify some, Mike said he could talk to his manager, who had given him the task. I asked him when he might do this. We were sitting across a table in a small meeting room. Mike had virtually collapsed in his chair and looked as if the air had been sucked out of him.

'I don't know that I want to go through all the trouble,' he said.
'Why not?'
'I am thinking of leaving the business.'
'You're thinking of this—or you've decided?'
'I am not sure.'

At this point I became really clear. Here was a highly intelligent and caring man who had given up. This was not a person acting to his potential. So I challenged him.

'Listen, if you don't get clear objectives from your boss you immediately eliminate one option from your choices—because if you're not successful in this project, you could lose your job. Tell me, how are you going to get clear objectives for the restructuring?'

Mike sat up and we talked through his options. When this part of the conversation was complete, I asked him how he would go about deciding whether to stay in the organization or not. Further action steps emerged. Mike left the meeting walking on air. Sure, nothing had been resolved, but he was now, to some degree, in control. I was unwilling to see him renounce his authority.

In challenging, it is particularly important to check your intent. 'Being right' at this moment helps no one. As I have said, a true challenge comes from a belief in another's potential.

Evoking creativity

Creativity is a vital part of coaching. It is what allows the player to break out of a difficult situation, invent a new future or possibility, and make a step-change in their productivity or quality of life. It shows up in many ways, but the two that we will focus on here are concerned with creating the future ('visioning' and 'goal setting') and innovation (new ways of doing things, new options). I describe a third technique, generating success criteria, later as part of the process of setting goals for a coaching programme.

In many of my coaching sessions, I am guilty of accepting what is apparently reasonable, in the sense of what could reasonably be achieved—for instance, when a player is creating a vision for their career. In my mind, I very often have an idea of what is possible for that person, or what he or she is capable of achieving. That set of judgments shows up in the session, and has the potential to limit it. What is even more worrying is that my idea of what the player is capable of is often greater than his or her own.

The same thing can happen in the options stage of the GROW model. The player comes up with a list of options within the confines of what is reasonable, and the coach goes along with it. Now, I am not an adherent to the school of thought that says you can have whatever you dream of. There are some things that limit us—at least in this stage of our evolution. But I am absolutely certain that there is much, much more available to us than we might think, if only we dare look.

I use the words 'create the future' with some resistance, because I know that there are people out there who think the world is the way it is; that their lot is either predetermined or delivered to them out of chaos. And they have an absolute right to that point of view. As a coach, I may of course challenge them on it. For their own sake, I would want them to be certain that it is a true belief and not an excuse that allows them to dodge responsibility and to accept the current situation without having to struggle.

This section of the book, then, is about how we can respectfully challenge players, and perhaps ourselves, to look beyond what is merely reasonable and scale the heights of the extraordinary.

Most of us, most of the time, create the future from the past. It is a predictable future. If we are brave, we may push the boundaries out a bit and create some 'stretch goals'. But, essentially, the future we imagine for ourselves is an extrapolation of what went on before. We create the future as a function of our previous experience: what worked and what did not work, our likes and dislikes, our strengths and weaknesses, our successes and failures. Unconscious processes also create needs that demand to be fulfilled. Parents, family, and cultural background all play their part—all from the past. You have to be strong and courageous to do something different—and that is after you have given yourself permission even to imagine something different. The funny thing is, the people who are supposed to have our best interests at heart are the people who do the most to ensure that we conform. 'But, dear, we have always thought you would become a doctor, just like your father. Why would you ever want to be a footballer?' (Why indeed?)

So is there another way of creating the future? Ultimately, not really, because it is nigh on impossible to imagine something that has not yet had existence. The only question is whether you are willing to be constrained by the past. Can you free yourself sufficiently to create a future that is worth hanging around for—one that demands your best efforts? You know what they say. Be careful what you wish for: you may get it.

Coaching techniques for creating the future

The first technique is the most simple: to create a vision. Agree a time frame that makes sense to the player (the end of the year, one year, five years, retirement). Ask the player to think of all the things that might be possible within that time frame. Ask him to suggest as many ideas as he can. When he has done that, ask him to edit the list down to the things he is willing to commit to.

A second approach is to have the player write a speech that would be given at the completion point of the vision: at retirement, at the end of a project, on New Year's Day. What successes and accomplishments would have occurred?

A third option is to have the player draw a picture of the vision. This can be either abstract, free drawing, or a more figurative image. Obviously, some people will find this kind of exercise easier than others. The player should then translate that picture into a written set of goals. Ensure he holds on to the picture too, however, as it will remain a potent symbol.
A final and perhaps least conventional option is to get the player to close his eyes and relax. Ask him to allow an image for the vision to come to him. The first image is usually the most useful. He can then either describe the image to you or draw a picture of it, as above.

Coaching techniques for evoking innovation

The following are three simple ways to have players move beyond what they think is possible and create some more innovative options.

Brainstorming is the simplest. Get the player to create a list of all the possible options. A somewhat less obvious method is to ask: 'If you had a magic wand what would you do?' or 'What is the most outrageous option you can think of?' or perhaps 'Think of something that would be impossible.' Identifying something that is apparently impossible can free up the thinking:

> PLAYER: It would be impossible for me to not do the project at all.
> COACH: What would be one step less than not doing it at all?
> PLAYER: Doing some part of it. Now that I say that, if I just did the initial assessment phase in the next week to ten days, my boss would be happy.

Transparency and the four tests

In completing this chapter on the skills of proposing, I want to remind you of the intent behind this skill set. It is to make available to the player the coach's observations, knowledge, experience, intelligence, insight, intuition, and wisdom. I mentioned earlier that these are the most difficult skills to deploy because of the inherent dangers of removing responsibility and choice from the player.

I am aware of two techniques that are helpful. One is the idea of transparency, which I also mention elsewhere in the context of building a good working relationship between coach and player; the other I call the four tests.

Transparency in coaching means that one's intentions as coach are completely clear to the player—explicitly so. Some examples a coach might use are: 'My intention in giving you this feedback is to help you understand the impact of your behaviour' and 'I really did not understand what you just said. Can you say it again?'

There is slightly different use of transparency that also helps when proposing. What I suggest is that you signal clearly to the player that you are moving from non-directive to directive coaching. This lets them know that you are aware that the information is yours, and that you do not wish to impose it. For example: 'I have a suggestion for you, another option; do you want it?' Assuming that he or she does want it, make the suggestion. And having proposed the option, return immediately to the non-directive: 'You had two options of your own, and then I added one in. Which is most interesting to talk more about?' The **four tests** operate in a different way. I will use them in a coaching session when I notice that I have something to propose such as a suggestion to offer or some feedback. If I am not sure that it is the right thing to do, I will ask myself the following questions:

- Will it raise awareness?
- Will it leave responsibility and choice with the player?
- Is the relationship strong enough to withstand the intervention (that is, is there sufficient trust in my intention)?
- What is my intent?

If the answer to the first three is yes and my intent is congruent with the suggested intent behind this skill set, I will go ahead.

Postscript

To finish this chapter, I offer a cautionary tale. Many years ago, I was coaching a senior employee—we'll call him Mark—in a large management consultancy. After the third meeting, I asked for some feedback. In responding, he made a request.

'I would like more from you,' he said.
'More what?'
'More input—more suggestions and feedback.'

I complied with the request at our next session, and by the end of the meeting was feeling quite dissatisfied. I could see Mark was, too, but on the day I did not have the necessary courage to ask for more feedback.

It so happened that the following day I had to give a demonstration of tennis coaching to a very discerning audience. I knew that if I made the slightest suggestion it would be picked up, so I was determined to be as non-directive as possible. It was a great session, and it reminded me of what constituted effective coaching. It also caused me to reflect on my coaching of Mark.

Taking a more directive stance had clearly not helped and, as I thought about it, I realized that in the earlier meetings I had been too polite with my questioning and had not helped Mark really clarify his thinking. In our next meeting, I listened even more intently and made sure that I really understood all he was saying. I applied the GROW model with more precision, making sure to establish a clear outcome from the conversation.

We finished our work in less than an hour—about half the normal time. Mark had worked so hard that he was almost perspiring. As I left the meeting room, Mark turned and said: 'That was hard work. You really made me think. Thank you.'

– CHAPTER 10 –

Understanding organizational context

No individual exists in isolation. Each person, each player, operates in a context, and for most people in business, that context is the organization. In chapter 11, I will put forward the notion that to be effective as either a manager—and indeed a coach—it is not sufficient to simply help the individual player become more effective—you must also ensure that the increase in effectiveness contributes to the achievement of the organization's goals.

Clearly, a large part of this is achieved through the coaching itself. ('Tell me, how will this course of action contribute to the organization achieving its goals?') But I am also suggesting that the capacity of the manager or coach to understand the organizational context in which the player is operating adds much to the coaching. This capacity might also be called consulting, the mention of which suddenly introduces a new, major topic. It is not my intent here to present a guide to consulting, however. What I do want to do is to give you two things: a holistic approach to understanding organizations, and an introduction to a critical skill: that of generating and testing hypotheses.

In diagram 5 (chapter 5), I identify one of the skill sets required for effective coaching as being 'understanding organizational context', and I suggest that the intent is to ensure that the coaching engagement meets the client's needs. One of the distinctions that I am at pains to make is between the player and the client. To remind you, the client is the organization itself, and typically there will be someone representing the organization—the person who pays the bill. The client's needs (or the organization's) will almost always be either different from—or greater than—the individual's, and in order for the coaching to be successful, these different needs have to be accounted for within the coaching intervention.

The four quadrants

There are two big themes that I want to bring together here in order to provide a lens through which you might view an organization. The first of these themes is the idea of inner and outer, and the second is the notion of the individual and the organization, which is developed further in chapter 11.

Bringing them together is most easily done visually. I draw a vertical line to show the inner/outer divide and a horizontal one to show the individual/organizational divide, thus producing four quadrants. This then suggests that not only does an individual have an inner and an outer ('belief' and 'skill', for example), but so too does an organization ('values' and 'performance management systems'). I will explain this diagram in more detail later on in this chapter.

In order to more fully understand these four quadrants, I have to take you back to the source (much as I would like to claim it as my original thinking). The four quadrants are presented in a book called *A Brief History of Everything* by Ken Wilber. He makes different but congruent distinctions to define the quadrants (as shown below). In the place of inner and outer he uses 'interior' and 'exterior', and in the place of organizational he uses 'collective'.

The four quadrants (adapted from Ken Wilber, A Brief History of Everything).

	INTERIOR	EXTERIOR
INDIVIDUAL	Freud (internal life) Truthfulness	Skinner (behaviour) Truth
COLLECTIVE	Kuhn (interpretation) Justness	Marx (collective social systems) Functional fit (justice system)

These are perhaps some of the simplest distinctions a human being can make: inside and outside, singular and plural. Let me try to bring this to life through a number of different routes. I will start by making some distinctions between interior (left-hand side) and exterior (right-hand side)

Interior and exterior

LEFT- HAND SIDE	RIGHT- HAND SIDE
Interior	*Exterior*
Subjective	Objective
Depth	Surface
Intentional	Behavioural
Mind	Brain

- **Subjective and objective:** The content of our experience that is subjective belongs on the left-hand side, the objective on the right.
- **Depth and surface:** Surface is on the right-hand side. Surface can be seen. Something exists; you can see it or feel it. Depth is on the left-hand side. It can only be revealed in conversation, and must be interpreted to be understood.
- **Intentional and behavioural:** Intention is about meaning and purpose (left-hand side); behaviour is what flows from that (right-hand side).
- Mind and brain A brain surgeon deals with the physical form of the brain (right-hand side), a psychologist with the mind (left-hand side).

Now I put back the horizontal line, and the individual/collective split shows the following points:

- Freud was concerned with the internal life of individuals (upper left), B.F. Skinner with the behaviour of individuals (upper right), Thomas Kuhn with how a shared, background context governs interpretation (lower left), and Karl Marx with collective social systems (lower right).
- **Truth** (upper right) is verifiable—meaning empirical truth, as in 'it's raining outside'. **Truthfulness** (upper left) is about trust—when I tell you it's raining outside, do you believe me? **Justness** (lower left), in the collective sense, is a commonly held context about whether something

is right or not. **Functional fit** (lower right), represents the justice system—that is, the framework of law and its process.

What this last point is intended to reveal is the idea that what occurs in one quadrant is reflected in them all. For instance, a community or nation's sense of justness needs to be reflected in the justice system; a disconnection here can cause much unhappiness, even outrage.

Wilber illustrates this connectedness with an example that I present here in my own words. Imagine an anthropologist visiting a North American Hopi Indian tribe and observing a rain dance. He would describe this objectively as a set of behaviours that have some function in the social system (lower right). A social psychologist visiting the tribe might enquire into the meaning of the dance and why it is valued in the community (lower left). Both investigators will arrive at different understandings, both of which are valid and, when taken together, add to the richness of the overall understanding.

As an aside, all too often we exclude one or other side from our understanding. B.F. Skinner held that one could never understand what was going on inside an individual—that the mind was a 'little black box', and that we should therefore not bother trying, leaving us with a literally one-sided behavioural psychology that has translated into a limited, carrot-and-stick approach to motivation in many organizations.

Let me stretch the analogy a bit further. Say one of our investigators picked on an individual participant in the dance and asked what the meaning of the dance was for that person (upper left). Assuming the individual was a healthy, engaged member of the community, the response might be: 'See the man leading the dance: he's my father and our chief. He's retiring at the end of the year, and I have to step into his shoes.'

For this individual, then, there is a meaning to the dance that is unique but also congruent with the collective meaning. What's more, the individual meaning will almost certainly translate into a different set of behaviours for that individual—he'll have to learn how to lead the dance (upper right). What occurs in one quadrant is reflected in them all.

The intention in the last few paragraphs has been to give you some sense of the richness of Wilber's work before I transpose the model into the organizational context.

The four quadrants: organizational version

	INNER	OUTER
INDIVIDUAL	Sense of purpose/meaning Aspirations Desires Attitudes Beliefs Personal values	Goals Plans Skills Behaviours
ORGANISATIONAL	Mission Culture Organisational values Corporate mindset	Vision Organisational goals Strategy Behavioural norms Code of conduct Performance management systems Management information systems

The four quadrants in organizations

- The upper left quadrant concerns the inner life of the individual: his or her sense of purpose, aspirations and desires, attitudes and beliefs, and personal values.
- The upper right quadrant is about the way in which the upper left manifests in the world: the individual's goals and the plans and strategies that flow from the goals. It also concerns his or her skills, behaviours, and even mannerisms.
- The lower left quadrant concerns the inner life of the organization: its mission, culture, values, the corporate mindset; what people believe is possible and not possible.
- The lower right quadrant is about the external representation of the

lower left: the organization's vision, goals, and strategies; the collective behavioural norms; the code of conduct. It also embraces the systems that facilitate the management of the organization.

In the same way as we extended our perspective from the individual to the team and now to the organization, it is to be remembered that the organization too sits within a context that is social and economic, meaning that the model can be expanded to embrace these things. I will limit our scope here to the organization itself in the hope of making the principles clear.

I said a little earlier that anything that occurs in one quadrant is reflected in all four, illustrating this with the example of the Hopi Indians. This idea provides two keys for using this model as a diagnostic tool to understand what might be going on in an organization. The first key is about presence: if I observe some aspect of the organization, then I must ask myself in what way is it present in the other quadrants.

The second key is congruence: for instance, an individual may have a desire or something he wants to achieve. The individual will need to take actions or have a plan (top right, outer individual) to achieve that desire. The actions or plan could lead him toward that desire, or away from it. The actions that lead toward the desire are deemed congruent with the desire. So, having observed something in one quadrant, you need to see how it occurs in the other quadrants, and then check that there is congruence. Be clear that this is no academic exercise—if it is not present, or is present but not congruent, failure ensues.

Imagine coaching an individual who has a need for acknowledgment (top left) that is expressed as a desire for promotion in the organization. Imagine, too, that he is acting and behaving (top right) in such a way that he is upsetting the people he manages and not achieving the performance goals he has set with his line manager. Looking at this through the lens of the four quadrants, you might notice the following:

- The actions and behaviours (top right) are not congruent with the expressed desire (top left).

- The actions and behaviours are not congruent with the organizational culture (bottom left).
- The individual goals (top right) are not congruent with the goals of the organization (bottom right).

Failure is imminent. As a coach, standing back and noticing these things is a vital activity. You might then choose to bring your observation to the attention of the player. I suggest how you might do that in the section below on hypothesizing.

Let me develop these ideas of presence and congruence with two illustrations. The first is a series of observations about the reasons behind why it is so difficult to change the culture of an organization, and the second is an anecdote—an illuminating one, I hope—about just such an initiative that was successful.

Most organizations today have some sort of statement about their corporate values, and in most cases these statements make absolutely no difference to what happens on a day-to-day basis. The four quadrants can help you understand why the values do not 'live'. Corporate or organizational values occur in the lower left quadrant. They are most often generated, or at least endorsed, by the leadership group in the organization. It is fairly easy to check whether these individuals 'walk the talk' (if the values are *present* in the upper right): that is, whether the leadership group behaves in a manner *congruent* with the expressed values. If they do not, the values are doomed from the start.

Now check whether the values are reflected in the performance management system (lower right). More and more, you will find that they are, but that they move on to the remuneration system , and again, in most cases, you will find that people are not specifically rewarded for upholding these values, and thus the values do not impact the day-to-day running of the business. Team working is something that you will frequently see in value statements, but that is not reflected in the pay packet.

The biggest reason why values fail to take root in most organizations, however, is the schism between the lower left and the upper left—between an individual's personal values and the expressed values of the organization. This occurs in two ways. Firstly, he leadership group that generated the values did not create them for itself but for *everyone else*, so of course they then don't 'walk the talk'. ('Teamwork is a good thing, but I'll run my department as I see fit.') Secondly, these values are simply imposed on most of the staff and bear little or no relation to the individual's own values. A failure to align the personal with the organizational prevents the values from coming to life.

Many years ago, I was part of a team that undertook a project with a leading retailer in the UK to create a shift in the culture. We designed a process that had coaching at its heart and which took the programme to each store and to each individual. The first step in the process was to get the staff to identify what was important to them—what made working in that store special? Only when this was done—once each individual had had their say—was the notion of values introduced and the executive team's values presented.

We then asked the staff to compare what they thought was important and special with the executive team's value statement. The congruity surprised everyone involved, but more importantly the values now had real meaning. What was in the lower left was reflected in the upper left. Of course, there was not a 100% overlap, but we had set up a communication channel to the executive that allowed for discussion about the differences, and in at least one case the executive reversed an earlier decision to charge customers for shopping bags—a decision that the staff thought inconsistent with both their own values and the values they thought the organization should hold. This dialogue was one of the critical elements in the programme because it confirmed that all parties were taking the matter of values seriously.

My second illustration concerns a consulting project that I was lucky to be involved in. Some years ago, I was given the opportunity by a consultancy to join a team working on a project with a large manufacturer of computer chips. A new factory was being built in Ireland, and there was great concern for the safety of the workers. Our task was to help create an injury-free environment.

In an early phase of the project, we held a workshop with the leadership group, which was made up of various representatives from the client: the management team, contractors, sub-contractors, service providers, and so on. We asked them to list everything that happened on site that was designed to increase safety. Long lists emerged: working procedures, emergency procedures, planning techniques, training, safety officer patrols, signs, barriers. When the items on the lists were plotted onto the four quadrants, there was almost nothing on the left-hand side of the page.

All of the activities and procedures were (and are) valid and vital, but this was only half the story. I remember in particular the recommendation for what should be done to stop workers from standing on the top rungs of ladders: paint them red (the ladders, that is). That's a right-hand side solution. But there was no enquiry into why workers would stand on the top rung when they knew it was dangerous. It also emerged that workers for one contractor would not intervene when they saw someone from another contractor doing something that was either obviously foolhardy or in contravention of the procedures. There was some unwritten rule that said you could not cross boundaries between employers, regardless of the potential cost—even if that meant someone's life.

While the procedures and training—all the things on the right-hand side—are important, they are useless if the left-hand issues are not addressed. Safety is predominantly about attitude and culture. When we started working on this project, the prevailing attitude to safety was that 'accidents happen'—in other words, they are not caused, so they cannot be avoided, and no one is responsible—and that 'they don't happen to me'. I recommend that you do not go onto a site visit with someone who holds these beliefs. Changing this mindset was the task before our team, and was therefore the thrust of our activity. For the record, after the completion of the project the company enjoyed the greatest number of hours worked without a significant injury in its history.

There is a vast richness in this model, and there are many ways of using it. It is a lens through which to view an organization. When working with an individual on a one-on-one basis, as either a manager or a professional coach, it is a relatively simple exercise to use the four quadrants to map out the details of each of the elements and to check for what is present and what is congruent. I have also presented the diagram to teams and had them complete it. However, it is most powerful when used in conjunction with the skills that I present in the next section: developing and testing hypotheses.

Generating and testing hypotheses

The example I gave earlier, of the individual seeking promotion, and the two that follow will, I hope, have shown how the four quadrants and the keys of presence and congruence can be a powerful diagnostic tool. Translating the insights or observations that emerge from using this tool into something that is valuable for the player and the organization in which she works is the subject of this section. This skill comprises generating and then testing hypotheses.

The ideas in this section are more obviously of importance to the professional coach, whose perspective of the organization from the viewpoint of an outsider—but with an intimate insight gained through coaching—should be a prized commodity by both organization and the coach himself. I would also argue that for any senior manager in an organization, a capacity to understand what is going on is a vital skill—not just for the development of his or her own career, but also for the organization itself, in terms of conversations about strategy, new products and services, and so on.

A hypothesis is a supposition or theory—a provisional explanation—developed from the available evidence or facts. The purpose of developing a hypothesis is to provide focus to attempts to understand an organization. Our purpose—as coaches and managers coaching their direct reports and seeking to understand an organization—is to ensure that the coaching is effective, and contributes to the organization achieving its goals. Once a hypothesis has been generated, the next step is to test it for accuracy.

In my earlier example of the individual seeking promotion, I might generate a number of hypotheses. It is important to note that a hypothesis does not need to be right. You also need to know that I have made up the following:

- The individual's desire is not clear to him. Is it about acknowledgment or just about gaining attention (at which he is succeeding)?
- The individual's values—which have given rise to his overtly and aggressively seeking promotion—are at odds with the organizational values, where patronage is the key.

I could now test my hypotheses in a number of ways:

- I could simply outline them to the player (as long as there was sufficient trust).
- I could develop a set of questions (for example: 'How do people get promoted here?') and ask people for their observations.
- I could keep the ideas in the back of my mind and see if more collaborating evidence emerged in further conversations.

It is worth pointing out that I almost never engage in one-on-one coaching without having spoken to the player's boss, their team, and other representatives of the organization. I do this for the purpose of understanding the organizational context of the player, and I do it by developing and testing hypotheses.

Here is a real example. I was coach for a short period to the leadership team in a small organization of international repute that was involved in the art world. This meant working with the three key directors on a one-on-one basis, and also with the three of them as a team. To start with, I spent some time meeting with various members of staff in an initial induction phase. As the coaching started, I found it very difficult to identify meaningful coaching goals with any of the three individuals. The first team-coaching session was very difficult, as nobody was willing to acknowledge in public that there were any problems. I was left with a real problem about how the coaching intervention could add value to the organization. As I thought about it between meetings, what I most noticed was the inability of any of the people I had spoken within the organization to tell the truth to me, to each other, or to themselves.

My initial hypothesis, therefore, was that for reasons that I had not yet grasped, straight talking and openness were absent from the organization, and thus there was no effective performance management, because feedback, and the notion of holding people to account (both of which require straight talking and openness), were completely absent. In order to test this, I fixed meetings with two people in the organization with whom I felt there was sufficient trust to have a more open conversation.

What emerged from these conversations was a singular fact: that the movement of many of the artefacts across international borders was, well, not entirely legal. In this environment, not only did people not want to communicate what they were doing, but also nobody—particularly the senior management—wanted to know. The secrecy required to keep this part of the business running infected the culture, and it became impossible to be open. I would like to say that I confronted the team I was coaching and they 'fessed up, but the stakes were too high. I did give them an opportunity to grapple with the issues by presenting a report of my findings, mentioning the culture of secrecy (but not my hypothesis about its origins, for I had no proof). The opportunity was well understood but not acted upon, and I was shown the door with great gracefulness. You win some, you lose some.

Not all situations are so dramatic, but in this case it would have been easy enough for me to continue with the coaching programme and to have added no discernible value, thus damaging my own reputation and sullying the good name of coaching.

Having established what I see as the benefits of generating and testing hypotheses, the key question, of course, is: 'How do I go about it?' In practical terms there are three stages in the generation and testing of a hypothesis: noticing, formulating, and testing.

Noticing, as I observed earlier, is the 'not trying' of thinking. In the 'inner

Generating and testing a hypothesis.

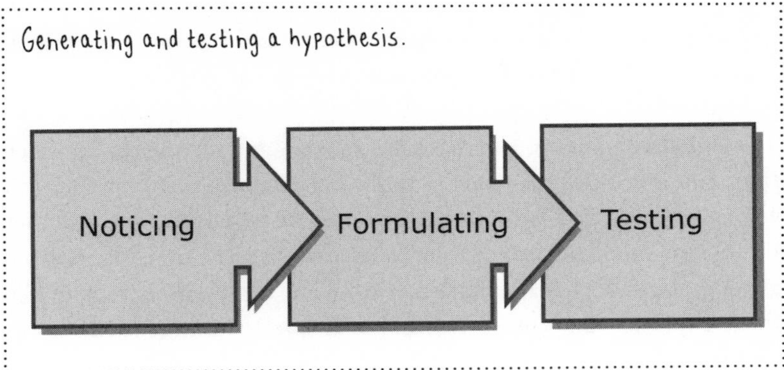

game' model, trying is a major interference. Trying to think hurts (you have to screw up your eyes) and seldom gets you anywhere. The best ideas come when you are relaxed, often while doing something entirely different. So simply take a step back and notice. Bring your attention to whatever thoughts you do have about the matter, the observations you have, your feelings—both emotional and sensory—to what your intuition is telling you, and to what you imagine or fantasize.

Formulate the shortest possible statement that brings together all that you have noticed. Identify all the possible sources of information that will help you test the hypothesis (people inside and outside the organization, documents, annual reports, industry reports, etc.).

Testing is best done by developing a set of questions (as in the example of the individual seeking promotion) from the initial hypotheses and then asking the questions of people who might have a useful perspective. Such people might include the player, their manager, their team, internal customers, the HR team, other colleagues, or consultants working in the organization.

A validated hypothesis can be used in a number of ways:

- If it directly concerns the player, it can be fed into the coaching conversation as part of the reality phase of the GROW model.
- It can be presented to the client for them to take forward.

- It can result in a proposition about how to rectify matters. For a professional coach, this could become another engagement.

This skill may appear to run contrary to the notion of coaching, in which the intent is to cause the player to think. I would hope that I have not put across a message that says coaches should not think or act upon what they think. That would be both pig-headed and foolish. If I have observations about a player or client's situation, it would be irresponsible to withhold them. I will refer back to this in the next chapter, on the art of coaching.

In bringing this chapter to a close, I want to state the obvious: this is not a book on consulting skills, and a few thousand words are never going to cover such a rich topic. But if I have conveyed the idea that individuals operate in a context—in this case an organizational context—and that it is necessary to investigate and account for that context in the coaching intervention or in the management of your direct reports, and if I have given an idea of how you might go about that, then I've done my job.

COACHING IN THE WORKPLACE

– CHAPTER 11 –

Coaching for leaders and managers

So far, I have covered the underlying principles, key models, and many of the skills of effective coaching, and I have tried to give a sense of what coaching looks like in practice. In this chapter I intend to show how coaching fits in the organizational context, and in the leader or manager's role. Crucially, I want to discuss how to use coaching to benefit the organization *and* the player.

Up till now, it has not been necessary to distinguish between the needs of the professional coach and those of the leader or manager. As we begin to think about coaching in the working life, however, it becomes necessary to distinguish between the two roles. So, in this chapter I will present most of the content from the manager's perspective. I have chosen to do this not only because it is the primary application of coaching (and there are more managers than coaches—just about!) but also because a professional coaches working in organizations needs to have a clear understanding of the manager's role, as most of the people they will be coaching are managers.

I also want to present an argument concerning the manager's role and the place of coaching within it. My desire to do so comes from a recent conversation during a workshop when I asked the participants—all managers—what the *purpose* of management was. Specifically, I asked this question: 'When whoever it was invented the notion of management, what was the problem they were trying to solve?'

I did not get a very good answer. Indeed, as we discussed it further, and notions of coaching emerged, one guy looked up and said: 'But this is not how I think of my job.' And therein lies the problem. Most managers think of their job in terms of their trade, discipline, or profession. The title 'manager' is thought of in terms of status and increased remuneration; it is not really thought of as an entirely new set of responsibilities.

My evidence for this assertion is the observation that few managers get out of bed in the morning and think: 'What can I do today to help my team be brilliant? That's just not what the job is as they see it. So, the argument that follows concerns the nature of management and the role of coaching within it, and it starts with some observations about a fundamental dynamic in any company: the relationship between the individual employee and the organization itself.

The individual and the organization

Individuals join organizations so that they can achieve some of their goals. These goals can be simple—to make enough money to pay the mortgage—or they may be complex—to satisfy a need to make a meaningful contribution. Equally, these goals can be well thought-out and clear, or reactive and ambiguous.

An organization employs individuals to fulfil its mission and achieve its goals. Typically, the goals are, if not clear, at least explicit, so those responsible seek employees who have the right skills and compatible values to fit in with those goals. Organizations are typically more diligent in identifying the right person then individuals are in identifying the right organization—or in understanding their own needs and goals.

A successful relationship between an individual and an organization is achieved when both parties achieve their own goals. This is a fundamental dynamic in any organization; if it is entirely neglected, people leave, and ultimately what that means is that there is no organization.

The individual obviously has a significant responsibility in ensuring the success of the relationship, as does the organization. The organization will give authority to a number of people to ensure that its responsibilities are met. Some of this is laid at the door of HR professionals, but by far the greatest share of an organization's responsibility rests with the manager. It

is his or her job to ensure that both parties' needs are satisfied.
There are three generic elements to the manager's role that enable this to happen: leadership, management, and coaching (see diagram).

The elements of the manager's role

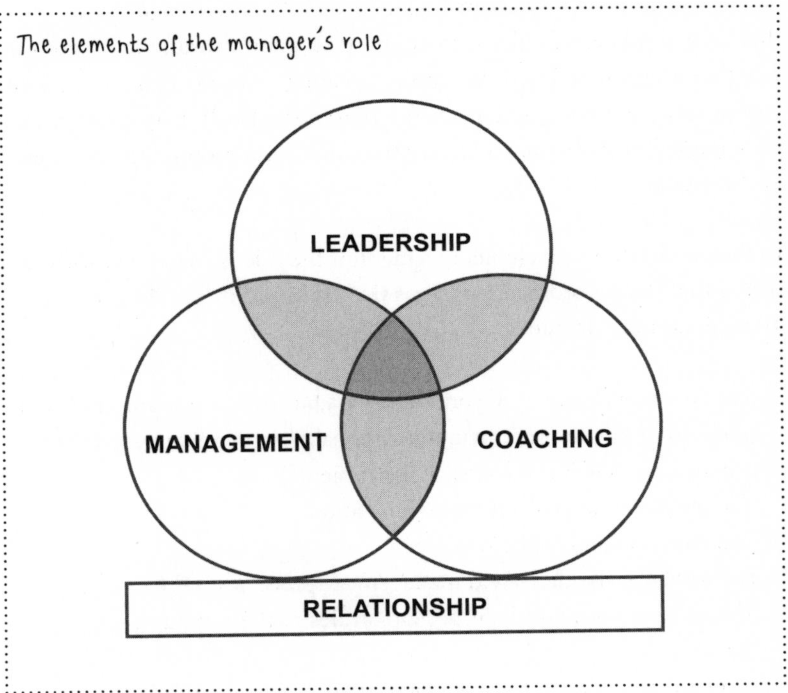

Leadership, management, and coaching

In the past 15 years, the notion that leadership is part of the manager's role has come to be accepted in most organizations. We—the world of business and management, that is—have separated out that part of the role and examined it, defined the component skills, written them into job descriptions and values statements, and created training and development programmes. Now what is emerging is that coaching is another critical element of the manager's role.

The evidence for this is to be found in the press articles, books, and conferences that have appeared in the last ten years, and in the ever-increasing demand for programmes to develop coaching skills. And so, in a similar way to how leadership has been distinguished from management, we need to separate coaching from management and leadership.

Much has been written about leadership, and I do not want to get into that discussion here. Suffice it to say, by 'leadership' I mean the part of the role that is concerned with the future: creating a vision, maintaining that vision, and identifying actions in the present that will deliver the vision. Role modelling fits here, too: living the values, and promoting the values of the organization.

In this model, the management element of the role is concerned with ensuring that the subordinate performs their role within certain parameters. These parameters include:

- The type and nature of the organization's business (for example, an employee of a kitchenware manufacturer cannot, on a whim, start taking orders for a new line of musical instruments)
- The purpose and goals of the organization
- The requirements of the specific job
- Performance standards and management processes
- The cultural norms and any accepted rules of the company.

In some organizations, perhaps where there has been an initiative to develop a coaching culture, managers have seemingly lost the right to manage; they can only coach, which often results in a loss of appropriate control and endless conversations on issues that are not negotiable.

As I have said elsewhere, coaching is the series of conversations that help a person perform closer to his potential, understand his role or task, learn what he needs to learn in order to complete the role or task successfully, develop the skills required for the next role, and, on a good day, achieve fulfilment—and maybe a little joy—at work.

In a workshop, I might ask the participants to identify all the day-to-day activities, interactions, and conversations that take place within the three circles of leadership, management, and coaching. Here is a typical list:

- **Leadership**
  - Conversations about organizational mission, vision, goals, values
  - Role-modelling behaviours, values
  - Inspiring and motivating.

- **Management**
  - Appraisals
  - Setting individual and departmental goals
  - Recruitment interviews
  - Creating personal development plans
  - Agreeing parameters of projects, tasks
  - Disciplinary meetings.

- **Coaching**
  - Conversations about how to deliver goals and plans
  - Giving feedback, making suggestions, offering advice
  - On-the-job training.

At a recent workshop, one of the participants, the sales director of a sizeable travel-agency chain, stood up and declared: 'I see, I have one management meeting a year with each member of my team to establish the goals, and the rest of the time I coach them to achieve the goals.' He did appreciate that this was something of an over-simplification, but he had understood the point and that he needed to invest a greater proportion of his time in coaching.

The partner in charge of a major regional head office of one of the big four (it may of course be three by the time you read this) accountancies learnt something different. He signed out of a workshop with these words: 'You may not have made my life any easier, but you have certainly made it more simple.' He realized that the conversations that he had avoided with his fellow partners concerning the clarification of their business goals (and non-performance in relation to them) were critical issues to the success of the office. He knew that he had a management task to complete—defining the goals—before coaching became possible. He also understood that he could not expect the conversations to be without friction.

There is an interesting paradox here. If people do not have clear goals, it is extremely difficult to be successful, and even more difficult to discuss performance. Forcing the issue—having the discussion, and being really clear about goals and what is acceptable and what is not—removes a mass of interference and the ill feeling that often accompanies under-performance, and enables best performance.

I will further develop this model of leadership, management, and coaching later in the chapter, but before I do that I need to introduce the notion of authority as it pertains to organizations.

The relationship

The final element of the model is **relationship**. All the other elements rest on this—if there is a poor relationship, no other meaningful conversations can take place. For a real conversation to happen, there needs to be trust. This is particularly true of a coaching conversation. The player must be able to talk about himself, his role, and how he goes about it with a degree of openness in which it is possible to acknowledge not only failures and shortcomings but also strengths and desires. Many of the skills of effective coaching are essential to building a productive, trust-based relationship—listening to understand and asking questions that follow interest, to name but two.

Organizational and individual authority

There is an underlying issue here that relates to these three elements. This is the issue of authority. By authority, I mean the power to decree something, by right or office, and to get it done by oneself or others.

In order to be an effective manager, it is imperative to understand the nature of authority and where it lies. Misunderstanding this issue will affect performance in a work organization, and is critical to a manager's capacity to ensure the satisfaction of both the organization and the employee. Here are some examples.

In the past (I hope!), the culture in most organizations was very authoritarian, 'command and control' being the predominant management style. Look at the words we use: 'subordinate' and 'empowerment'. How I hate the latter word. People are by their very nature powerful. That we have to 'empower' them suggests that their power has in some way been diminished or taken away.

We have—through our culture, institutions of state and religion, and particularly our educational systems—trained people to submit to authority. And there are consequences. Under a strongly hierarchical, authoritative 'regime', people do not take responsibility, do not take risks, are not creative, and are not proactive. They wait to be told. This is not how to get the best from people—'our greatest asset'. This is misplaced authority.

On the other hand, many people do not understand that when they join an organization, they sign up to play that organization's 'game'—to play by its rules. I know this because very few people take the time in the recruitment phase to understand the organization they are joining. The closest most people get to making a real choice is to select a profession or particular industry to work in. Otherwise, the agreement around the pay package or salary is about as far as it gets.

Again, in most cases, this is perfectly understandable. You've left school, college, or university, and you have debts to pay off. Perhaps you have a family, or a mortgage. Pragmatism is the only operable philosophy. It works because the money is sufficient to make it worth staying. So you get on with it, do as you're told, and are able to pay the bills.

Clearly this is not true for everyone. But the point I am trying to make is that most people do not 'stand in their authority' and take responsibility. The consequence of this is that people experience little fulfilment at work, and are thus difficult to motivate and perform with mediocrity.

I remember giving an address to a conference. The delegates were all senior managers and executives, mostly male and heading toward middle age. These were people who were used to exercising power, with many of them controlling budgets of millions of pounds. I asked them who made the decision about where they took their holidays that particular year. There was a short pause, and then an embarrassed laugh—no, a giggle—ran around the room. These guys exercised absolutely no authority about how they were going to spend two or three weeks of the year (weeks that they had probably fought hard for in negotiating their salary package). And most of them had travelled to places that would not have been their first choice, and done things they would not join a queue of two for. And they had not even come to a compromise on the matter—they had simply capitulated, in the name of a quiet life.

Organizations can assume too much authority, and individuals too little, although there is a spin on this. I notice that the generation that is currently entering the workforce has a completely different relationship with authority from the one that I, for one, had. They are more assertive, assume more 'rights', and are less willing to 'toe the line'. This in itself is a compelling reason to adopt something other than a 'command and control' management style, because in a world where attracting the best staff is increasingly an issue, the best will not stay in an unduly authoritarian organization.

There is an appropriate balance to be struck between individual and organizational authority, and the manager, caught in the middle, needs to understand how to strike it. Sometimes, individuals get together with other individuals and agree to share authority so that they can achieve something together that they cannot achieve apart—like a marriage. And in order that it is successful, the individual parties have to surrender some of their authority to the whole. Similarly, organizations and individuals can get together. It's a business relationship called employment.

Individuals have authority. By this, I mean that there are areas of their lives where they can make decisions and execute them without reference to others. Organizations have authority, too. They can declare the business they are in, establish goals and strategies, and execute them.

One way to understand how the matter of authority impacts on organizational life is to draw a vertical line through the middle of the three overlapping circles shown below. You can then begin to see where this balance lies. The left-hand side of the line represents those things that are the concern of the organization: its needs, aims, and objectives. On this side of the line the organization has authority. When you join an organization, you sign up to that authority.

The area on the right-hand side of the line represents those things that are the concern of the individuals: his needs, aims, and objectives. On this side of the line, the individual has authority.

The elements of the line manager's role, classified according to authority

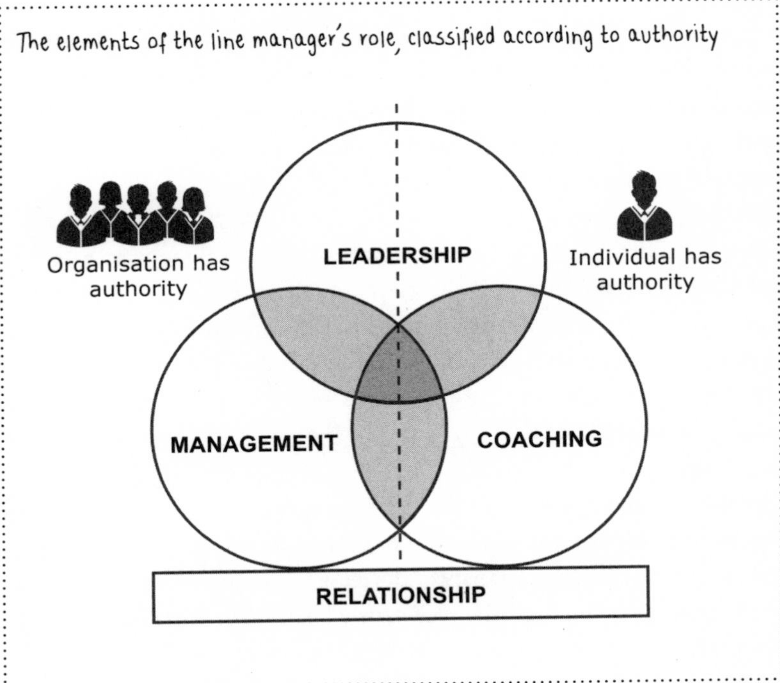

It is overly simplistic but nevertheless useful shorthand to suggest that *what* an individual employee does sits on the left-hand side in the authority of the organization. Clearly, this is best agreed—with the manager using coaching skills to understand the individual—rather than decreed.

How the what gets executed sits for the most part on the right-hand side of the line, in the authority of the individual employee.

Let me draw a parallel with the game of tennis. When a player stands on a tennis court, he implicitly signs up to the rules of the game as laid down by the International Tennis Federation. The player cannot change the size of the court or the height of the net, or alter the rules. He cannot, for instance, decide to kick the ball. If he does, the game ceases to be tennis.
In addition to the player, there are a number of other people on the tennis court: his opponent, the umpire, the coach. The umpire and the coach are of interest in this analogy, not the opponent. The umpire's role is essentially about compliance. It is his job to ensure that the rules of the game are adhered to. In this sense, it is analogous to the management element of the of the manager's role. The coach's role is different. His job is to ensure that the player gives his best performance and learns and improves from one match to the next. And this is obviously analogous to the coaching aspect of the manager's role.

The very different roles of the umpire and the coach suggest a different kind of relationship with the player, and different corresponding behaviours. The umpire's relationship is invested with authority, as decreed by the governing body. It is a directive, command and-control, interactive style, and appropriately so, for if the rules were not enforced, there would be no game.

The coach's relationship with the player is altogether different. The content of the conversations between the coach and the player concerns matters that are within the authority of the player: whether he hits a backhand with one or two hands on the racket, or whether he adopts an aggressive serve-and-volley strategy or a backcourt, counter-hitting approach.
On the right-hand side of the diagram, where the individual has authority, instructing or telling that individual is less effective than listening to him and asking questions such that he comes to his own solution or insight. This is the fundamental reason why coaching is predominantly a non-directive activity.

The word 'authority' can give us an insight here. It has the same Latin root as the word 'author': a writer, someone who creates. The root is *auctum*, which means, among other things, to produce, to increase, to cause to grow, according to the *Shorter Oxford Dictionary on Historical Principles*. An author writes his own book. A manager dictating the book to be written would soon wear the patience of the writer, turning him into a mere scribe, thus destroying his motivation and, in time, his very ability to be creative.

In the past, the failure to distinguish between managing and coaching elements of management has caused a kind of leakage. Managers try to handle performance and learning with a management style—command and control—rather than a more facilitative style. This derives from the fact that, for most people, those they have encountered who have been charged with helping them perform or learn effectively have also had a management responsibility.

Teachers teach, but they also ensure discipline in the class, and at certain times pass judgment on their pupils' efforts—judgments that dictate the immediate future. This is true for managers, too. And for the most part, neither professional has recognized that the style appropriate to the one works less well for the other. One leaks into the other. The umpire and the coach in the tennis analogy have it easier, as the role is split between them; the manager, however, has to 'wear both hats'. There is a school of thought that proposes 'managing with a coaching style'. Many articles have been written around variations of the idea of 'The manager as coach'.

This is another form of leakage. In one company that I know of, it is almost impossible for a manager to give a direct instruction to a member of staff—they have to coach. I think this is just clumsy or incomplete thinking, and it can have the effect of undermining the manager—and, ultimately, coaching itself. It is important to separate one circle from the other.

Interestingly, when we distinguish between both sides of the vertical line, the management element takes up less time; when you place authority where it mostly belongs—with the player—the need to manage diminishes. It does not go away, but it takes less time.

There is, it seems, a somewhat worrying corollary of this. Some years ago, I ran a workshop for the UK management team of a well-known fast-food chain with the intent of introducing them to coaching. The workshop was difficult; there was a level of polite engagement but no passion, which is unusual. It was only afterward, when I reflected back on the event, that I saw what had happened. From their perspective, you see, there is only one way to cook a burger; quality (if that is what you call it) and consistency are everything. The 'shop floor' culture—one of managing, not coaching—had engulfed the leadership team.

Clearly, if there is little or no need to coach, there should be little or no coaching; in some jobs, standardization is key to success. The problem here was that the leadership style had become very directive, resulting in a culture where risk was avoided and innovation suppressed. It is difficult for such a business to diversify.

These ideas on authority also relate to the third circle—leadership—where the line down the middle retains its validity. Sometimes, it will be appropriate for a leader to make a clear and unequivocal statement about a direction to take, or to take a difficult decision without referring to others. At other times, he may adopt a more facilitative, coaching approach to a leadership issue and elicit a decision from others.

In summary let me suggest that there are a number of issues to be borne in mind for a manager:

- Managers need to manage, and have a responsibility to both the employee and the organization to do so.
- Managers—as part of managing—need to agree clear goals for their direct reports (*what*). Interestingly, while this is clearly a management task, using coaching skills to identify the goals in the first case is always more effective.
- Managers need to hold their direct reports to account for the goals that have been agreed.

- Once the goals have been agreed, and any other parameters surrounding their role such as values and behaviours, the manager coaches the direct report to achieve the agreed goals (*how*).
- Managers need to lead, keep present in the minds of their direct reports the overarching aims of the organization, and be role models for the desired values and behaviours.

I remind you of the ideas of flow in chapter 5: you can see that management that embraces leadership, management, and coaching can help create flow. Some of the conditions of flow are as follows:

- There are clear goals every step of the way.
- There is immediate feedback to one's actions.
- There is a balance between the challenges and skills required.
- Action and awareness are merged.
- Distractions are excluded from consciousness.
- There is no worry of failure.
- Self-consciousness disappears.
- The activity becomes autotelic.

If you are reading this book from the perspective of a professional coach, you need to understand these guidelines and ensure that, if it is relevant to the objectives agreed with the player, he or she also understands these issues. The notion of authority in organizations is also important for the professional coach. The coach needs to understand that the organization is the client, and that it therefore has a right and responsibility to influence the goals for any coaching intervention. The coaching itself—which will focus mostly on how to achieve the goals—is in the authority of the player, and thus remains confidential.

Introducing coaching into an organization

The skills involved in coaching can be applied in many different ways and in many different environments, from the workplace to the schoolroom to the sports field. As you internalize the skills and make them your own, you will find that they show up in many aspects of your life.

One of the exciting things about training people to coach is watching the participants progress through the programme and report at the various workshops how what they have learnt has shown up in all areas of their lives: the consultant who was having a difficult meeting with a client, and who was inspired to change the meeting into a coaching session; the director of training who found herself listening to her husband; the senior executive who began acknowledging the real talent and creativity his teenage daughter possessed.

For me, these are some of the more inspiring stories, not because they are so important and meaningful—which they are—but because they give a tangible demonstration that something has changed at a very fundamental level in the participants. These stories signal a shift from an earlier approach that was founded in the need to be in control, to be right, to fix, to heal, to make better—pick any of these—to one that acknowledges the extraordinary capacity of human beings, and in which the primary skill is simply removing interference.

This, however, is a book about coaching in the workplace and there are obvious applications for the skills, which are useful to examine.

Some coaching happens in a rather formal fashion. There is a clear and explicit agreement to coach between the coach and the player, and it typically happens offline, outside normal work activities. Coaching also takes place in a more informal way, as part of the general run of play. It happens between colleagues at all levels in the organization, between peers, between a manager and direct reports. And it does not respect hierarchy. I remember asking a former boss, just before a critical meeting, what his ideal outcome from the meeting was. One successful meeting later, he acknowledged the value of the question, and how it had helped us retain focus in the meeting.

Informal coaching does not necessarily require a clear agreement between coach and player, although most relationships work better when the parties know what is expected of them. Informal coaching happens on the spur of the moment. In the canteen, a colleague indicates that he is having a difficult time with a particular client or with some aspect of a project; a member of staff complains that he will never get the job done on time. Both of these are opportunities for coaching. The conversation described in the opening chapter was just such an opportunity—one that could have been missed, and that Henry initially dismissed with the words, 'It's bound to get better.'

The possibilities for increased performance, for learning, and for innovation that have been lost in this way are beyond number. When training people, in some workshops we get the participants to pair up and to give three-minute coaching sessions. They are always surprised at how much can be achieved in such a short space of time.

This three-minute exercise was developed with a client in the USA—an international strategic-management consultancy—where the only coaching you got from your partner occurred as you held open the door of a taxi. It became known as 'kerbside coaching'. I have renamed it 'corridor coaching', partly because that would seem to present more opportunities (not subject to the weather) and partly because of the desire not to be associated with other kerbside professions.

It is in situations such as these that the manager who coaches shows up most clearly and can have a profound and lasting effect on the performance and learning of his direct reports. And, frankly, it is a significantly more rewarding way of doing business. When this happens, an organization truly has a 'coaching culture'. As the HR director of an international beverage producer and distributor observed: "This is not about Innovation with a capital I in our business but rather about hundreds and hundreds of innovations—small i—all across the organization, in every conversation.' The remainder of this chapter discusses some of the principal applications of this, again presented from a manager's perspective.

Manager coaching direct reports

The most obvious of all applications in the workplace is that of a manager coaching those who report to him or her, be it in a formal or informal sense. This book, and in particular this chapter, is a plea to take the coaching element more seriously, so that the player performs more effectively, learns, and get some fulfilment.

As I said earlier, coaching where there is a management relationship presents some difficulties in that the manager has explicit power, in the face of which it can be awkward to create an environment of trust. Another difficulty is that the player may simply want to be directed or may not want to have to think for himself and to take responsibility. These difficulties are not insurmountable, and some of them are addressed later in the section headed 'Obstacles and pitfalls for the manager'..

Coaching in the management processes

Most organizations have a number of management processes that lend themselves to coaching, in particular such people-management processes as performance reviews, appraisals, development reviews, objective-setting meetings, and progress reviews. It staggers me that there are still organizations where the manager sets the direct report's goals. I can think of few quicker or more sure-fire ways to erode motivation and undermine responsibility.

Thankfully, most modern organizations are more enlightened than that, and allow for self-assessment on the part of the subordinate, and for employees to identify their own goals. Both of these processes provide perfect opportunities to wrap coaching around management processes. Think about the really critical conversations—the ones that have significant impact in organizations: conversations to set objectives, to agree budgets, to establish or review projects. Now imagine if these conversations were 'redesigned' as coaching conversations.

Take the budgeting process. The direct report is sent off to prepare a budget. After a while, he comes back with his best effort, and is told to strip out 10% of the costs—and what about the new product launch? There's another iteration, and probably another. In this process, time is wasted, enthusiasm is eroded, and the relationship between manager and direct report is undermined. And there is little or no learning.

With effective coaching, this would be less likely to occur, thus providing a great boost to organizational effectiveness.

Coaching during major change

Among the most debilitating side effects of major change—be it organizational or cultural—are fear and uncertainty. This results in large numbers of people looking for answers to an array of questions, usually from the leadership group.

Adopting a coaching approach has a number of benefits. Firstly, it has the effect of putting ownership and control back into the hands of the player, and this can lessen anxiety. Secondly, in change situations, where there are often no right answers, coaching will draw out possibilities and options from which the best can be selected. Thirdly, it gives some respite to the leaders, as others begin to take responsibility and join in the game. Leaders can't—and shouldn't—do it all.

Before and after training events

Coaching can be used to great effect to ensure that someone gets full value from a training programme. The manager or trainer can coach a delegate prior to an event so that he is very clear about his learning objectives. When the event is completed, a further coaching session can consolidate the learning and ensure that it is effectively applied in the workplace. There is evidence to suggest that the effectiveness of training can be increased by the order of 25% in this way.

Coaching as part of leadership

Effective leadership is so dependent on the personality of the leader, the culture of the organization, and the nature of the business that I am not going to be foolish and make a broad statement about good leadership. What I will say is that when there is an alignment between what inspires an individual, the job he or she is doing, and the direction of the company, people at all levels can give their best freely, communication becomes easier, and phenomenal results can be reaped. A coaching approach that directly involves staff in the direction the business take and the shape of individuals' jobs can be part of what creates that alignment.

Coaching can also be used to gain buy-in to organizational values and behaviours. For instance, working with a player to identify her own values and then helping her relate these to the organization's values—and therefore discovering which elements are congruent and which are not—will bring the values to life in a meaningful way, particularly if there is room for debate—and influencing—around those elements where there is discomfort.

Coaching on projects

Coaching is a great way to go about delivering projects within time and within budget. It is very similar to coaching teams, so I refer you to chapter 14.

Coaching upward

'Is it possible to coach my boss?' is a question frequently asked at coaching skills workshops. The answer is that anyone can be coached—if they are willing. What is interesting, I think, is what is behind the question. Usually, the underlying question is: 'How can I change my boss's behaviour?' To this question there is a different answer: you cannot change anyone else's behaviour—only they can.

What you can do is give them some feedback. If they are willing to hear the feedback and understand it, then coaching may be appropriate—after the feedback has been given. He has the right to choose his coach, which may or may not be the person giving the feedback. In my experience it is unusual for a boss to be willing to be coached by a subordinate, although it is not unheard of. When it does happen, it is a tremendously powerful signal that the boss is truly open to learning and meaningful communication, the impact of which extends well beyond the person who volunteered the feedback in the first place.

This scenario fits into my loose definition of formal coaching. Coaching upward in the informal sense can happen much more easily and frequently, but is dependent on the prevailing culture within the organization, and on just how much of a control junkie—or how desperate—the person 'upward' of you is.

Coaching peers

Coaching between friends and within a peer group is perhaps the easiest environment in which to coach in the sense that there are the fewest obstacles to an effective relationship. This is because it is less likely here than in a management relationship that there are competing agendas, or that the coach has an investment in the outcome (other than that the session should be successful, which is an obstacle in itself).

Some organizations have instituted a system of 'buddy' coaching or co-coaching. The notion here is that two people who have some training in coaching skills support each other in the pursuit of performance or learning objectives. As you might imagine, some of the pairings meet once or twice and then the pressures of work override the initial good intentions. Other pairings maintain the practice even when the individuals move on to other parts of the business, or to other countries, resorting to phone conversations for their coaching fix. I know of at least one case where the buddy coaching relationship has persisted after both protagonists have moved to new companies.

Mentoring

In principle, mentoring is concerned with longer-term career issues, while coaching is concerned with more immediate performance issues. The point to be made here is that the models, tools, and skills that are critical to coaching as I have described them will also make a more effective mentor.

A mentor who is reliant on, say, an avuncular style and dependent on having had significant experience of the organization, business, and life may well provide great benefit and be a wonderful person to be with. At the very least, however, such a mentor would need to be able to listen effectively in order to ensure that the pearls of wisdom were indeed pearls in the eyes of the recipient. On a more positive note, a mentor who has vast experience and can use it to good effect—and who can also employ a non-directive approach when appropriate—will have much greater impact.

There are many other opportunities to use coaching outside the workplace, and although they do not fit in with the topic of this chapter, here seems as good a place as any to note them.

Coaching your partner

'Don't do your professional stuff on me.'

I have heard those words a few times, and not without justification, for coaching a partner can seem intrusive and patronizing. Effective coaching requires that there is a relationship in which the coach can divorce (there's a joke there, somewhere) him or herself from the outcome, and from what is going on for the player. But when two people have a commitment to each other, and their lives have become entwined, such a separation is often difficult to achieve, and sometimes virtually impossible.

While it is important to acknowledge that there are some quite tough obstacles before the use of coaching within, say, a marital relationship, it is not impossible, and an ability to do so may even be a sign of a healthy and mature relationship. The key is to identify and talk about the obstacles before doing any coaching.

Coaching children

Coaching other people's children is almost the easiest of all applications, and the most fun. In my relationship with my stepdaughter Victoria, my coaching skills have played an important part—particularly when it comes to homework, as I have already indicated with the 'overdue essay' story in chapter 5. In general terms, when she gets stuck with something, the truth is that she probably knows more about the topic than I, so helping her think it through is the most valuable assistance I can give. (I also happen to believe that homework is for her to do, and not me, so if I use coaching, she gets to write her own essay and use her own prolific imagination.)

Coaching and the skills involved have a wonderful place in the relationship with children. In the teenage years, where nothing seems to work, the least you can do is listen. I will not pretend to have always been successful in this domain.

Coaching yourself

In a sense, you are coaching yourself all the time. When you take your nose out of this book to ponder something—be it a new insight, or a disagreement you have with something that I have written—one could argue that you are coaching yourself. When you take time out to consider a project you are engaged in, or ask yourself whether something is really coming together as you wanted it to, you are coaching yourself. Some of the most valuable time that I spend on behalf on my own clients is when I take the dog for a walk—I just have not yet found a way of charging for it, although I guess I could set the dog's expenses against my tax bill.

There are limitations, however, to a person's ability to coach him or herself. Coaching is about raising awareness. If I consider an issue on my own and in isolation, at a certain level I will be trapped by my own patterns of thought. From the inside, I cannot see me. Part of why coaching works is because, in that moment when the player communicates to another and is understood, the thoughts are externalized, and a certain distance is achieved between the player and his thoughts and emotions. Think back to the analogy of the man in his car in the traffic jam in chapter 9. He is now on the bus, upstairs on the front seat, just noticing.

There are techniques you can use to externalize your thoughts and achieve some objectivity. For instance, a former colleague tells the story of an argument he had with his wife. At some point, in desperation, he left the house and, as he put it, 'let the front door do the talking'. Once outside on the pavement, he brought his breathing into focus and relaxed somewhat. He then proceeded to coach himself.

Feeling inspired, he did the following. He walked first on the left-hand side of the pavement, and from this position—this physical place—he was the coach, asking the questions. Having asked the question, he then moved to the right-hand side of the pavement, from which place, as player, he answered it. While this made life difficult for other people wanting to use the pavement, and proved upsetting to the neighbours who must have thought him to be drunk as he weaved his way around the block, my colleague did get to some resolution.

Another technique that works quite well is to write your thoughts down on paper, using the GROW model to structure the ideas. Opportunities to coach are all around us. I suggest you start by simply noticing them, and then, when you have the right permissions, take them: they are opportunities for achievement, fulfilment, and joy.

– CHAPTER 12 –

Starting to coach as a leader or manager

Learning the skills of coaching is a relatively easy task, and in a workshop situation most people can achieve a level of skill in a few days. The problems arise when they get back to their places of work—where business, the prevailing culture, and the expectations of co-workers, the boss, and direct reports tend to undermine the good intentions expressed at the end of the workshop.

In this sense, then, this is one of the most important parts of the book. Of course the skills are important, but I suggest that even a relatively unskilled coach whose heart is in the right place is a lot better than someone who gives no coaching at all. Now that I think of it, I am not sure it is possible to be a 'bad' coach if your heart is in the right place; a solid 'inner game' spawns a solid 'outer game'.

This chapter comes in three parts. The first is intended to show how a manager might introduce coaching to his (as yet) unsuspecting direct reports; the second covers the same ground, but for the professional coach. The third part is relevant to both manager and coach, as it looks at building an effective coaching relationship, and at setting goals.

I gave a lot of thought to where to put the section on goal setting. I have decided to put it in this chapter because it is so fundamental to the relationship—without a clear purpose, the relationship falls apart—and because a clear focus is such a crucial element of effective coaching in the workplace.

The following options are not the only ways of starting to coach direct reports. They are simply methods that have been tried and tested by participants on the programmes at the School of Coaching. Many of them can be used together. I am slightly concerned that this section will seem repetitive of those elements of the previous chapter that describe where coaching fits in the manager's role. The intent here is different from that, however. It is to suggest how specifically one might begin.

Through the appraisal or performance review

The obvious place to begin coaching is in an appraisal or performance review. The manager will use coaching skills to define and agree objectives and success measures, and the outcomes from such events will include a set of objectives for the player to pursue—most of which will be suitable topics for coaching. The foundation for ongoing coaching is thus set, and continues in monthly one-on-one meetings. Many people I have worked with have an item on the agenda of their monthly one-on-ones with their direct reports that is entirely at the discretion of the direct report. As trust builds, underlying issues that impact on performance are often brought up, such as self-confidence or relationships.

You may have gleaned from this that I believe it is a matter not just of 'best practice' but also of critical importance to have regular one-on-one meetings between a manager and a direct report. This method has an advantage over many other ways of introducing coaching in that the prospective player will have experienced coaching already in the meeting, and will have some sense of what they are letting themself in for.

Using feedback as the starting point

This is another easy and uncomplicated way of bringing coaching into the workplace. To introduce coaching in this way requires that there is some real feedback to be given, and that it is substantive—by which I mean that it is not something the receiver of the feedback can change simply and immediately.

Assuming those two requirements are in place, once the manager has successfully given the feedback he or she can then offer support in the form of coaching. If the coaching is seen to work, it is a relatively simple task to introduce other topics onto the agenda, and thus establish an ongoing coaching agenda. The feedback can be given as part of a regular series of one-on-one meetings, or it might arise from a specific event. In either case, the manager is indicating that a change is required, and is offering to support the direct report in making the desired change. I refer you back to chapter 7 and the section on giving feedback for additional information.

Through a team agreement

This is a very powerful way to introduce coaching, because it involves making explicit agreements in public that are thereafter more difficult to ignore or forget. It assumes that the manager has a team of people reporting directly to him, and involves bringing the team together for a meeting that, at a minimum, would have the following outcomes:

- A collective understanding of what coaching is, including the notions of non-directive coaching and formal and informal coaching.
- Agreement about how and when coaching will be used.
- The ground rules for coaching. This should include an agreement about confidentiality, and may also include discussion about how topics are added to the coaching agenda, timing and frequency of one-on-one meetings, formal and/or informal coaching, and how to give feedback.

It is a good idea to demonstrate coaching during the meeting with a willing team member, as this is the most direct way of communicating what coaching is. The volunteer player must choose a real topic to be coached on, otherwise the demonstration will not work. The beauty of this approach is that it allows for open discussion about the effectiveness of the coaching approach and the manager's proficiency.
There are two additions to this approach:

- The meeting can be facilitated by an external coach, which allows the manager to participate fully.
- This meeting—and subsequent follow-up meetings—can start with giving feedback to the manager on their coaching.

The following are possible agenda items for such a meeting:

- Describe the purpose of the meeting and the desired outcomes.

(A coach would also ask if the group wanted any other outcomes.)

- Define coaching. A good approach is to get the team to share their individual experiences of effective and ineffective coaching, whether that coaching took place in work, in sport, or at school or university. The definition of coaching given earlier might also help.
- Demonstrate a coaching session. First describe the GROW model and then demonstrate with a willing volunteer. It is a good idea to identify the volunteer beforehand, and to make sure that he or she has a real issue to be coached on. Set a time limit for the session: 20 minutes is about as much as most spectators can manage. After the session, review it with the group.
- Discuss with the team what the applications of coaching might be. Out of all the possible applications, agree with the team the ones that are appropriate, and how the team might get started.
- Ask what ground rules would help make the coaching effective. Make sure that the issues of confidentiality and feedback to the line manager are discussed.

Through an individual agreement

It follows, of course, that pretty much the same approach that I have described for introducing coaching via teams can be used on a one-on-one basis. It implies a fairly formal coaching relationship. This would work well with someone whose performance is poor—or equally someone with very stretched goals. The initial meeting in the coaching programme outlined later in this chapter describes how to get one-on-one coaching started in detail.

Alongside tasks, projects or change programmes

Introducing coaching in order to assist individuals or teams achieve important tasks or projects or to see through the delivery of a change initiative is arguably the most successful route to implementing coaching. It makes it clear that coaching is not some new trend in the organization. Rather, it puts coaching in its proper context: performance and learning. At the time when the individual or the team is being offered the new task, the manager can offer coaching support.

Obstacles and pitfalls for the manager

As an activity, coaching is really rather simple. But that does not mean that coaching is easy. With a little bit of discipline, most people can learn to listen, and the GROW model is hardly rocket science. The difficulties, such as they are, often lie outside the skills. Here are two prime examples of obstacles and pitfalls that line managers may have to face in trying to establish an effective coaching relationship.

When the direct report does not want to be coached

The first rule is this: if someone does not want to be coached, attempting to coach will get you nowhere. If an individual in a work organization is achieving all of his goals, is not disrupting things for others, and does not want to be coached, leave him alone. If, on the other hand, he is not achieving his goals but still refuses coaching, the manager needs to be really clear that this is no longer a coaching issue and has become a management issue. Most organizations have a well-established process for handling these situations, and that is the province of the HR department.

When openness and judgment clash

Many years ago, I had a conversation with my then manager about my sales performance. The performance itself was not the issue, although it could have been better; it was that I hated making cold calls to prospective clients. We had a brief conversation about this that I took to be coaching. Some six months afterward, at the annual performance review, I made my case for an increase in salary and for promotion. This was rejected because, by my own admission, I was not good at selling!

As I pointed out earlier, the manager wears two hats; one (managing) requires making judgments about another's performance that have significant impact on the other's pay and prospects; the other (coaching) requires them to create an environment where the player, the direct report, can be open and vulnerable. Incompatible, you might think. Maybe not.
I suggested earlier that it was difficult to coach one's partner. I suggested this once at a workshop, and I was picked up by a participant. 'Not impossible—there's just a lot of interference' was the response. The ability both to coach and manage another requires a strong, honest relationship,

with clear performance goals and success measures, thus bringing as much objectivity as possible to the assessment of performance.

– CHAPTER 13 –

Coaching for coaches

This section is not about how to establish yourself as a professional coach. That's another book, and there are other people better qualified to write it than I. It is about how a professional coach, whether an external or internal agent, delivers value over time to the player and the client—that is, the organization in which they work.

My approach to this is to describe a coaching programme. In doing so, I am indicating a formal relationship that takes place over a period of time and that is designed to help the player achieve substantial goals. Such a programme has a number of elements that I will describe in some detail. Not all these elements will be appropriate for every situation, so this is really a pick-and-mix affair. To tell the truth, I have probably never run a coaching programme that included all the elements described. What actually occurs is a far more fluid and natural process. But all the elements have their place, and I believe it is important therefore to understand each of them, not least because they collectively represent a wonderful checklist (see diagram below).

Initial meeting

Purpose: to establish whether there is a need for coaching, achieve agreement in principle, build relationship and establish the ground rules.

1 After formal introductions, the coach suggests the above as the purpose of the meeting.
2 An easy starting point is the player's background. This might include an overview of his educational and professional history, and a description of his current role.

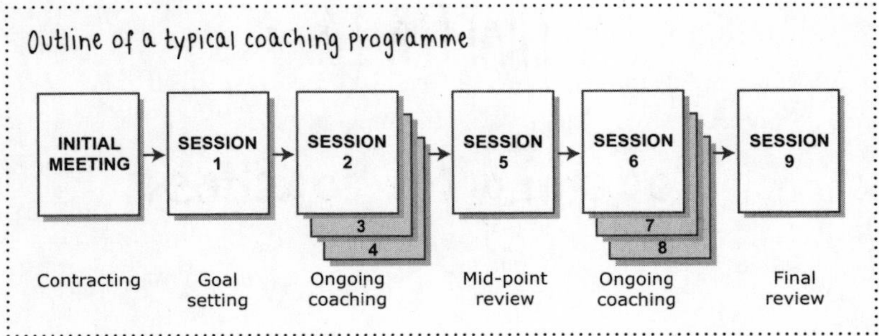

3 The next talking point is probably about why coaching is on the cards, what prompted the introduction, and what the player is hoping to achieve through coaching.
4 The conversation then shifts to what coaching is, possibly introducing the GROW model, the spectrum of coaching styles, and a description of a typical programme.
5 At this point, there will be an emerging sense that coaching is either the right way to go or not. If not, have the courage to say so, and support the player in finding what he or she need.
6 If it does seem appropriate, then a discussion about the ground rules for the programme is next on the agenda. Issues to cover here include confidentiality, honesty, openness, feedback to the coach, and logistical issues such as venue, the duration of the programme, and potential postponement of sessions (how many hours' notice, and so on).
7 Seek a commitment to go ahead. Remember you have to make a commitment, too, and that you need to feel confident in your ability to deliver on your part of the bargain. If you are not confident, try to identify the obstacle and, if appropriate, address it with the player.
8 With an agreement to proceed in place, the coach should talk through the first session (outlined below) to identify any materials or information required.
9 If the client for the programme (he who pays the bills or has commissioned the coach) is not the player, the coach and player should discuss how the client is to be kept informed (see 'Public and private goals' later in this chapter). It is always best that the player is responsible for this, thus protecting the trust in the relationship.

Session one: establishing context and programme goals

Purpose: to identify and agree specific goals and success measures for the programme such that the needs of the player and the client are met.

1 The coach declares the purpose of the session and asks the player if he has any additional goals.
2 Given that the player's needs do not change the nature of the session, the coach starts by asking the player what his goals are for the coaching programme. This may duplicate part of the initial meeting, in which case check that the goals have not changed. Then bring into the discussion the various sources from which goals might emerge:

   - The client's perception (that of the HR manager, for example)
   - The player's manager's perception
   - Feedback to the player
   - The player's current business objectives
   - The player's career vision
   - Recent appraisals, performance reviews, or personal development plans
   - Strategic initiatives and change programmes in the organization.

   All of the above may inform the player's goals. The feedback to the player can come from sources such as any existing 360° survey, interviews conducted with the player's direct reports, and the line manager.

3 The next step is to identify the success measures for the programme. I will suggest how to do this toward the end of this chapter.
4 If there is a requirement to keep a third party—such as the client or the player's manager—informed about the coaching process, sending a copy of the goals to that individual for agreement and input is an appropriate step. It may be that there will be a set of public goals as well as one or two private goals shared only between the coach and the player, where the issues are of a more personal nature. This is a legitimate practice, as long as the coach and player are agreed that the achievement of the private goals contributes to the player's productivity in the client organization.

5 The final step might be to check that the goals identified are achievable in the time frame of the programme, and in the number of sessions contracted.

Session two (and subsequent sessions)

Purpose: To make progress toward the programme goals.

1 The coach declares the purpose of the session—in words less formal than those above—and asks the player what he wants to achieve in it. While a principle of coaching is 'following interest', it is important that the topic(s) for the session are considered in relation to the goals for the overall programme. It is often all too compelling for the player to choose a topic that is, literally, the last thing on his mind—a recent insight or upset—and not deal with the issues that will take him toward his longer-term goals.
2 With the topics for the session agreed, the actions from the previous meeting are reviewed.
3 With that done, work through each of the identified topics using the GROW model.
4 The penultimate step in the session is to pull together the action plan.
5 The final step in any session is to request feedback from the player. This is important not just for the learning of the coach but because it demonstrates a commitment to openness, builds trust, and develops the relationship, making it possible for the player, in turn, to be open and trusting.

Mid-programme review

Purpose: To check progress toward the programme goals and review the coaching relationship. Ideally the mid-term review will form the first part of a typical session, leaving time for some coaching in the meeting.

1 Progress toward the programme goals is reviewed, ground rules are reviewed, the effectiveness of the coaching is discussed, and feedback from the player is solicited. Sometimes, players are reluctant to give feedback, often because they do not want to upset the coach or run

the risk of damaging an important relationship. In order to move beyond this, I find that if I reflect on the sessions before the meeting, I can usually identify a number of issues that I am not comfortable with in my own performance. If the player is not forthcoming with feedback, I can ask specific questions, and this will break the deadlock. On a longer programme, it may be appropriate to seek feedback on the player's progress from other parties, such as the client, his manager, his direct reports, or other colleagues or peers.

2 Time permitting, other topics are identified and worked through, and an action plan agreed.

Final review and completion

Purpose: To assess progress toward the programme goals and complete the relationship.

In the final session, it is important to take the time to review the programme. This allows both the player and the coach to maximise their learning from the event and to complete the relationship. Relationships that are incomplete—that drift into separation—retain some of the emotional energy that was invested in them.

This energy is not available for other relationships or activities. For instance, if the player cancels a session and then the session is not re-booked, the coach may spend a considerable amount of energy wondering what went wrong, or whether he was doing a good job. It might even undermine his confidence. The player, on the other hand, may be embarrassed about it or feel guilty, and spend time worrying about what he is going to say when he finally meets up with the coach.

The outline for the session is similar to the mid-programme review as outlined above. If the client and the player are different people, the client should be included in the process of completion. The coaching may end at this point, or a different relationship may emerge, such as quarterly meetings, in which case return to square one and resume the programme as outlined above.

I like to finish coaching relationships by helping the player to identify the specific things that they have learnt during the course of the coaching relationship, as it is typically these lessons that are the legacy of the coaching, rather than the goals achieved. This also works against the possibility of the player becoming dependent on the coach.

The contract

It is useful to have a clear, written contract with the player. There is also a need to have a contract with the client—the organization—and this is best expressed in the public and private goals matrix (as described at the end of this chapter).

You do not want to be too heavy-handed with this and to present it as if it were a legal document, or for either party to feel constrained by it. The purpose of the contract is to ensure an effective, hassle-free relationship—and, like any contract, you will not need it until you do. At that point, if you do not have one already, it is too late. It should include the programme goals and success measures, the ground rules, and, if appropriate, the fees.

Meeting duration and frequency

There are no set rules about the frequency and duration of meetings, and each coaching relationship will develop its own pattern. The place to start—as you might guess—is by asking the player, but there are some other factors that should also be considered in developing a programme:

- The time frame within which the goals are to be achieved
- The player's need for support
- The level of stretch in the goals.

I find it very difficult to get anything meaningful done, when coaching in the formal sense, in anything under an hour, and as such I will usually book a one-and-a-half or two-hour session. This is also driven by the fact that I am not on site in the way most managers are, and I want to make sure that the sessions are complete. If the coach and player work in the same building, it is easier to reconvene or catch up between meetings.
At the beginning of a coaching relationship, meetings tend to happen

more frequently—fortnightly, say—and then change to a three-week or monthly pattern. This is because players tend to need more support in the early stages, as they consider making changes and begin to implement them.

An example of a meeting report

MEETING REPORT

Name	David O'Hara
Organisation	Network Bank plc
Coach	Myles Downey
Date	23/5/03
Meeting no.	6

TOPICS DISCUSSED

We reviewed the Actions from meeting 5. The only outstanding action was the conversation with Gerry to clarify the purpose and parameters for the Axis project.

We also reviewed the overall goals for the programme. The only major change we agreed was to change the priorities. You felt thatthe performance – and support of – your direct reports had become more important as this should free you up to look to longer term matters.

The performance of your direct reports became the principal topic for the session. You identified 'three levers' that you have available to improve performance and give more support

- re-visiting each individual's performance goals so that there is greater clarity and that the priorities are agreed
- giving accurate feedback on performance to date (in the past you have tended to avoid potentially uncomfortable situations)
- re-establishing monthly meetings with the individuals and the team where there is a specific slot for your direct reports to bring up their issues

Finally, we spoke briefly about how you might approach the next executive meeting. You have been given feedback that you are seen as too confrontational by your peers. At the next meeting you will try two things

- being very clear about your intent in making any intervention and telling your peers what it is
- taking a little more time to understand each contributor; asking questions, etc.

NEXT ACTIONS

Hold meeting with Gerry.
Write and send an e-mail to your direct reports about how you intend to improve performance and increase support.
Get Tessa to book team and individual meetings for the next 6 months.

NEXT MEETING

10th June, 8.30am at your offices.

Meeting reports

Meeting reports are documents that contain the vital information from a coaching session. At a minimum, this should include the topics discussed, the key points, and the actions arising from the discussion.

There are two main schools of thought that I know of in relation to meeting reports. One school has it that the coach should write up the meeting; the other (not surprisingly) advocates that the player should. In both cases there is agreement that having a record of what was discussed and agreed, together with the action points, is a necessity. The argument for having the player write up the notes is that in the writing, the player will achieve another level of clarity and responsibility. When the coach is external to the organization, and providing a service, then perhaps the coach should complete the meeting report.

I have taken to using a pre-printed sheet (see above) which I fill in before the end of the meeting and then photocopy, leaving a copy with the player and keeping one for my own records.

Practice players

There is another sense in which 'getting started' is important for the professional coach. Inevitably there is a moment, before you become a professional coach, when you are an apprentice or a novice.

To build confidence and to iron out any flaws in your approach, one option is to adopt what the School of Coaching calls 'practice players'. This comes before you take on your first paying client. People learn coaching most effectively when two factors are present: the player is addressing real issues (role-playing does not work, as the player can keep on inventing new circumstances, and there is no 'truth'), and the learning environment is safe. This takes the pressure to perform—to 'get it right'—off the coach, and sets the scene for more relaxed coaching sessions in which the coach can get good-quality feedback from the player.

Outside of a workshop, the best way to establish these factors is to work with practice players. Practice players are people with a real interest in being coached, and who understand that the coach is still in training. The notion of 'real interest' means that the person is committed to getting value from the coaching, not just engaging because he or she is a good person and wants to support the novice coach.

This is also a powerful way for a manager to introduce coaching while continuing to learn. Maybe all sessions should be viewed as 'practice sessions' by the coach, because it removes the interference called 'this is important/serious', and in an atmosphere of mutuality and playfulness such as this, both parties make the most progress. I notice that coaches often feel that they have to do it 'right' and that they cannot make mistakes. What nonsense. As long as I have a strong relationship with the player, I should feel free to try new things and get it wrong—all in the service of the player and the client. If I do get it wrong, I just need to acknowledge it and try again.

Obstacles and pitfalls for the professional coach

While the issues raised in this section are of particular importance to the professional coach, they can also crop up for the line manager.

When the player is seen to be failing

It is very difficult to coach successfully in a 'remedial' situation. I use the word remedial very deliberately, because that is often how organizations—or people in organizations—react when a staff member is seen to be failing. One of the reasons people fail in organizations is because the organization has let them down.

Of course, I do not want to take the responsibility away from the individual. If an individual is failing, they need to accept responsibility for that and take some action. But in any relationship—and here I include the relationship between a staff member and an organization—there is 100% responsibility for the relationship on both sides. (Yes, I do know that that makes 200% in total.)

There are two reasons in particular to be cautious:

1 The organization may have already rejected the player but not admitted it. In this case, even if the coaching is successful, the organization may be unable, or unwilling, to readmit the player.
2 The player may have already rejected the organization, but again not yet admitted it.

I have frequently been called into situations by clients where a player is deemed to be failing. The problem is often that the player has not been given the feedback early enough—if at all—or that the manager has been unwilling to bite the bullet and have the difficult conversation. So they get the executive coach in to sort it out. The most useful thing that can be done in these situations is to get the manager, or the HR department, to have a frank conversation with the 'failing' employee, so that all parties know where they stand. After that, coaching may be possible, but I would want everyone to know that a possible outcome from the coaching is that the player might decide to leave the organization.

Who is the client?

Whether you are an external executive coach or a manager, when you engage in coaching, you need to be very clear as to who the client is. Many people—particularly external coaches with a background in the psychological professions, where confidentiality is all—believe it to be the person they are coaching. It may sometimes be the case that the player and the client are the same person, but usually they are separate.

The client is the organization or its representative—the person paying the bill. And the client has rights, too—the right to have an input to the goals of the coaching, so that the player can deliver these in line with the organization's needs. This problem is in part resolved by the use of the public/private goals matrix at the end of this chapter, in part by the coach's capacity to understand the organization's need, and in part by the integrity of the coach and the player.

It's not therapy

Sometimes it seems to me that a good listener creates a vacuum—a silence—that others feel compelled to fill. And as the speaker notices that what he is saying is not being evaluated or judged, he begins to trust. So he says some more—things he would never dream of saying under other circumstances. The things that taxi drivers have said to me when I have been sitting quietly in the back of their cabs, listening but not judging, are beyond belief—and, in some cases, beyond repetition.

It happens occasionally in coaching sessions, too, that the player broaches a topic—because he trusts the coach—that may well be better handled by a counsellor or therapist. If this happens, the coach should abandon coaching, but—please—not listening, and refer the player to a counsellor or therapist.

The coaching relationship

Effective coaching rests on a solid relationship between coach and player. It seems such an obvious thing—too obvious to have to write it down—but the truth is that the only thing that can cause coaching to fail is an insufficiently strong relationship. As a practising coach and a supervisor of other people's development as coaches, I notice that almost every unsuccessful coaching intervention is the result of a ropey relationship.

In the skills matrix in chapter 5, I refer to the skill set of 'building relationship' and describe the intent as being 'to create an environment in which the player feels safe and un-judged'. Without a relationship, there is no coaching. In fact, the only real mistake a coach can make is to damage the relationship irreparably. Everything else is recoverable. Coaching fails when something is left unsaid, or even when the player feels he has to leave something unsaid. The relationship has to be sufficiently strong for the player to trust in the coach. The player has to feel comfortable saying whatever is on his mind, to own up to mistakes and weaknesses, to suggest the absurd or the impossible—in a word, to be vulnerable. The player must feel free to challenge the coach and to give feedback, to say 'This isn't working' or 'I don't understand the question', or 'No, I don't want to consider that option yet—this one is more interesting.'

I want you to be clear that to have a good coaching relationship does not necessarily mean that you have to like the player. Sure, it helps, if the two of you are going to be locked away in a room together for an hour or more, but that is not what does it. Care, or more specifically love, does it, and I can care for someone that I do not like.

The practical, mechanistic aspects of establishing a good coaching relationship have been dealt with earlier in this chapter. Here, I would like to discuss what underpins that relationship. As you will see, the relationship foundations are all manifestations of caring. A willingness to listen and understand is also key.

The qualities of a good coaching relationship include the following:

Trust

The player needs to be able to fully trust in the coach. He need to trust that his thoughts, beliefs, fears, and ideas will be respected and not ridiculed; to trust in the coach's intention to be of real assistance. And to trust that the information elicited in the session will not be divulged to others.

Equally the coach needs to be able to trust in the player. To trust that the player is fully engaged in getting value, to trust that he or she is being as truthful as is possible. I have occasionally found myself in a coaching relationship where the player was participating because it would look good to his superiors, demonstrating a willingness to change when it is in fact far from the truth. As soon as I detect this, I will gracefully confront the player. Two things tend to happen at this point. Sometimes, the coaching ends there and then, but with the relationship intact (OK, almost intact), or the individual chooses to engage for real.

Honesty

The player needs to be honest in the sense of telling it as he really sees it or believes it to be, and in taking responsibility for his actions, perceptions, and beliefs. And the coach needs to be honest with the player. This is more difficult, because a player will occasionally ask for the coach's opinion—and the opinion is likely to include some judgment or assessment.

Judgment and assessment do not fit easily with a non-judgmental, non-directive coaching style. And yet there is a need to be honest. So, if the coach is asked for an opinion, the first thing to do is to find out why the player requires it. Very often, asking why the player wants your opinion will allow the player to see that he was looking for reassurance—and, once that has been understood, he may no longer require your opinion at all.

Another tack is to turn the request back to the player, as in: 'I'll give you my opinion if you want it, but before I do, tell me what your own point of view is.' If, after both of these questions, the player still wants the coach's opinion, the coach might choose to give it. I am usually quite willing to express a point of view on a plan of action, an idea, or behaviour. I would resist responding to a question such as 'What do you think of me?' and challenge why the player wanted to know. After all, this is just my 'stuff'—my judgments—and has no real validity or currency.

Openness

Openness is critical in the coaching relationship, and coaches need to recognize that this is the hardest-earned factor in relationship-building—even more so than honesty. Coaching requires complete honesty, but only *appropriate* openness. So there is a judgment call to be made.

Appropriate openness means that all the information the player possesses—all the thoughts, ideas, and beliefs required to make progress on the topic—are available and part of the discussion. Other things need not enter into the sessions, however, if they are not needed to make progress. It is likely that the player will have thoughts, ideas, and beliefs that he would never reveal to anyone—let alone a work colleague—or may simply have promised confidentiality on an issue. If a situation arises in which the player is unable to be open, and this is explicit—that is, if the player is honest about it—then that in itself is a sign of a healthy relationship. He just may need to find another coach—or a counsellor—for that particular topic.

Transparency/intent

We touched on this already in chapter 9, in the context of proposing effectively. Transparency means that one's intentions, within the context of the coaching, are completely clear to the other party—and, almost certainly, explicitly so. Transparency is a quick way to build trust in a relationship. As a relationship develops, there is typically less need for it to be present explicitly, because the partners trust each other's good intentions.

Transparency in a coaching session, coming from the coach, sounds like this:

'My intention in giving you this feedback is to broaden your understanding.'
'I really did not understand what you just said. Can you say it again?'
'I need to understand this part better. Can you tell me about it?'
'I am really sorry, I lost concentration ...'
'I'd like you to try this visioning exercise. I believe it will help clarify what you really want.'
'I have a suggestion for you. Do you want it?'

In the name of transparency, I introduce new clients to the GROW model and the spectrum of coaching styles in the first meeting, so that they know what I am doing in the session. To better understand the importance of transparency, just think how not understanding the coach's intentions would impact on the player. I suggest that he would find it difficult to trust the coach, and to be honest and appropriately open. No coaching.

Setting goals and defining success criteria

This section could reasonably have been included in chapter 9, but because the quality of the goals and success measures that are agreed at the beginning of a coaching programme is the single greatest factor—after the relationship—that impacts on the success of the coaching, it seems to me to fit well in the present chapter.

Setting goals

Many readers will be familiar with the acronym SMART. This suggests that goals should be specific, measurable, achievable, and realistic—and in a clear time frame. These are useful guidelines and all goals should be measured against them. Here, I want to talk about different types of goals and to link them on a matrix.

The matrix has three main vertical columns. The middle column (from which I tend to commence my coaching sessions) is for performance goals. These describe what the player is seeking to achieve during the course of the coaching programme or the term of the coaching (for example, a year where the manager is the coach). A professional coach will draw on the annual goals that the player has agreed with the line manager to start off this column.

Programme goals matrix

PROGRAMME GOALS

PLAYER	COACH	START DATE	COMPLETION DATE
Sean O'Driscoll	Myles Downey	3.10.03	3.4.04

	LEARNING GOALS	PERFORMANCE GOALS	SUCCESS MEASURES / BEHAVIOURS
PUBLIC GOALS	To be able to write compelling proposals for $50,000 and over	To deliver $250,000 sales in the first half-year	Receipts totalling $250,000 filed Rewards to sales team for each sale of $50,000 and over
	To revisit recruitment skills notes	To build a 'sales machine' for the Southwest region capable of sales of at least $1.5m	Two new sales executives recruited Sales tracking system designed and installed on intranet
	To learn how to facilitate effective sales team meetings (keeping the focus on results)	To build a strong sales and sales support team	Information shared No divide between backroom and sales staff Energy and fun in the office
	To brush up coaching skills		Regular get-togethers (every 2 months)
	To learn how to plan a large-scale project	To deliver the Chameleon project on time (organisational responsiveness)	Project team in place by May Project parameters signed off by Board in July
PRIVATE GOALS	To learn how to identify and present information that Mike (boss) requires	To establish a solid working relationship with Mike	More trust, he keeps me informed Regular meetings (fortnightly) Agreement about how he involves himself in Chameleon
	To be better able to structure presentations	To build own self-confidence	To feel able to speak up at Board level To enjoy public speaking

The column on the left is for learning or development goals. I will often find the content for this column by asking: 'In order to achieve your performance goals, what do you need to learn?' Another question that is useful here is: 'In order for you to achieve your longer-term goals or vision, what do you need to learn?'

The right-hand column is for success measures or specific behaviours that the player wants to adopt. Success measures, which I will talk about next, relate directly to the performance goals, and the question might be: 'When you have successfully achieved your goal, how will you know?' New, desired behaviours can emerge in their own right, as a result of feedback, or as a function of cultural change in the organization. The matrix itself has some good examples. Clearly, you can start with any column, following the interest of the player.

Public and private goals

I have noted already that the client—the organization, or the payer of bills and salaries—has some rights, and that clients needs to know that the outcomes of the coaching are in their best interests. However, the player may wish to keep some goals private and confidential with the coach. I am thinking here of issues such as self-confidence and difficult working relationships—with the player's manager, for example.

To satisfy both of these needs, the matrix is divided in two by a horizontal line. Above the line are the public goals. These can be communicated to the player's manager and a representative from the HR department for their input and agreement. This is a process that I strongly recommend, as it increases the effectiveness of the coaching through having higher quality goals and can ensure that the player is given feedback that might otherwise be missed. Below the line are the private goals. As a matter of integrity, these must contribute to the player's performance within the organization, as the coaching is being paid for by the organization, and takes place during working hours.

Generating success criteria

Let me tell you the story of Kevin. I was coach and manager at a small tennis centre in Ireland that was situated beside a large housing estate. The estate had been built on the outskirts of the city to house a former inner-city community. The community's old housing had been torn down to make room for office blocks and shops. As with many such developments, the uprooted community developed more than its fair share of problems. There was a high rate of unemployment, plus the attendant problems with violence, drink, and drugs.

On one particular Friday, shortly after the schools had broken up for the summer holidays, a boy of about 12 years old appeared at the tennis centre. He watched everything that was going on and gravitated toward the court where I was working. I was coaching a client in the serve. All the balls had been hit down to the other end of the court, and when I turned to collect them I almost tripped over the boy. He had collected all the balls into the basket and brought them back to me. Without a word, he then ran back to the other end of the court.

Some minutes later, all the balls had been used up, but the client needed to quickly hit some more. I looked to the boy, who was at the other end of the court. He took a ball and threw it the length of the court straight into my hand. I said nothing, put the ball in my pocket, and held out my hand. Thwack. Another ball, straight into the palm of my hand. I looked at the client. This frail-looking boy, with a great big grin, had an elegance of technique and a rhythm that you seldom see. His name was Kevin. He had played tennis once before, with an aunt. He had enjoyed it, and he wanted to try again. He spent the rest of the day helping me during the lessons.

The next day, we had a tennis lesson. Kevin learnt very quickly. It was a Saturday and there were a lot of people about. Pretty soon, there was small crowd around the court. It was not just that he had talent and a grace of movement, he also had a joy about him that was infectious. By the end of the summer, Kevin had made remarkable progress. He had also seen some of the better tennis players in his age group working out at the centre.

The following year, Kevin wanted to play a few tournaments. I agreed to coach him over the winter, and in exchange he agreed to keep part of the centre tidy. In making our agreement, I asked him what his goals were. He wanted to qualify for the national championships and win a first-round match in the next year. That would have put him in the best 32 players in his age group—a stretch goal if I had ever seen one.

Kevin worked hard over the next year, often coming to the centre before school for extra practice. The tennis centre had never been so tidy. Unbelievably, he qualified for the nationals. I had a business meeting when his first-round match was on, so I did not get to see it. I got to the club just as the result was posted. He had won. It took me some time to find him, but when I did, he was in an annex to the changing room. He had been crying.

'What's wrong?' I asked. 'You won, didn't you?'

'Yes,' he replied, his voice shaking.

'So what's wrong?'

'It was a bad match. I felt tense the whole time. We were both angry—I could see it in his face. And I used a bad word. And he called me a bad name. I don't want to play like that.'

'So how do you want to play?'

He relaxed a little. 'I want to feel relaxed and calm, like when we play.'

'What else?'

'And I want to feel the ball in the centre of my racket. I want us both to be happy, smiling. And I want be able to say "good shot" when he hits a good shot.'

'Is that how you want to play your next match?'

'Yes.'

Kevin lost his next match. But it was a great victory for him. He played beautifully, and he gave full expression to who he was.

Kevin's original goal was very clear by most criteria. It was specific, measurable, realistic (if a bit of a stretch), and had a clear end date: to reach the second round of the nationals by the following year. But we had missed something critical, and had stumbled onto an interesting additional technique in resolving it.

When Kevin told me what had gone wrong and then translated it into how he wanted it to be, everything was described in terms of things that he could see, hear, or feel. When you think about it, if you cannot detect something through your senses, it does not exist. It is a figment of your imagination.

If you take the time to translate goals or objectives into what you can see, hear, and feel—and smell, too, if you must—then you will identify two additional aspects of the goal. This technique is invaluable when filling in the third column of the programme goals matrix.

In a coaching session, it might sound like this:

COACH: So what is your longer-term goal for your time-management?
PLAYER: If I could get to a position, within the next month, where I am saving three hours a week, processing less paper, and getting the weekly reports out on time, that would be just great.
COACH: And when you have successfully achieved that how will you know? What would you see that would be different?
PLAYER: Three times a week I'd get home earlier.
COACH: And what would you see? What would be the evidence?
PLAYER: The evidence would be me: my body, standing in the kitchen, with the clock saying six o'clock and not seven.
COACH: And what would you hear?
PLAYER: I'd hear the kids laughing and playing, because they would still be up. And, on a good day, my wife saying: 'You're home early, that's nice.' And she'd be happy to see me.
COACH: What would you see, actually, if she was happy?
PLAYER: A smile.
COACH: And what would you feel?
PLAYER: More relaxed.
COACH: How else would you know?

Making a goal or objective as 'real' as the example above gives some clear measures—confirmation that it is the right goal and typically deepens the desire to achieve it. I suppose it is appropriate that a chapter on getting started should finish with observations about goals and success measures, for the only real measure of the effectiveness of coaching lies in the achievement of goals.

In coaching, 'getting started'—the initial sessions where the goals are agreed, a contract formed, a relationship of trust begins, and the organization's needs are accounted for—can feel like a somewhat tedious part of the process. But overlook it at your peril, for it is the foundation of a successful relationship.

— CHAPTER 14 —

Coaching teams

So far in this book the attention has been on the coaching of individuals. It does not take much imagination to begin to wonder how this approach, and these skills, might affect teams. Many organizations have invested time and money in developing teamwork in the hope that it will increase performance. No doubt there will have been some benefit to the bottom line in some cases, but the vast majority of team-building and team-development exercises flounder when the raft they have built hits the rapids. The 'outward bound' approach almost never translates into the workplace, and 'high-performance teams' become so dependent on 'process'—doing it the right way—that it leaves the individual's needs and the task itself behind. OK, you can stop waving your hands—of course there are exceptions. But in the main, the learning, such as it is, is not sustainable.

Coaching teams has a very specific intent: to ensure that the team achieves its goals. Any activity or exercise that the team undertakes must contribute to this and thus the organization's goals. Some years ago, I worked with a team that had been established to launch a new financial service. It involved the building of an entire organization, from the people to the systems to the office buildings. This is team coaching at its most exciting—where it involves the delivery of tangible goals.

If coaching individuals has its difficulties and complexities, then these are multiplied when coaching teams, putting a new spin on all that has been discussed so far in relation to coaching individuals. I am talking about the obvious distinction between individual and team coaching: there are more people involved.

At the surface level, this means that more time is spent in the process of coaching. An individual can get to a level of clarity and make a decision relatively quickly. In a team, that process takes much more time, as each person needs to be heard, disagreement needs to be handled, consensus and commitment need to be built. Now, look beyond the surface, look to the interrelationships in the team, the dynamics, and evolution of the team, and a whole new ball game emerges.

These issues should not scare you off coaching teams because, as will become evident, there is an inherent resource unique to teams that can produce a form of 'self-coaching'. This resource is the very human desire to be in communion. As I see it, this is a sort of 'team self two'. In this state, a team can achieve extraordinary goals with minimal effort.

This chapter, then, is about the inner aspect of teams. I identify some of the interferences that can occur in teams and suggest a number of ways of eliminating them. The final section is about team dynamics. This may seem like something of a detour, but when you understand in an inner-game context, I believe you will realise that these dynamics represent an unconscious drive toward team self two, and as such it represents a valuable tool in team coaching.

It is important to point out that an exclusively inner-game approach is as flawed as an exclusively outer-game approach. Clear goals, roles, and processes (outer game) are also required. As a colleague eloquently put it: 'You're half-assed no matter which cheek you're sitting on.'

The inner aspects of teams

Gallwey's initial explorations into the inner game concerned individuals and identified the extraordinary capacity of human beings to get in their own way—self-interference. He observed that the single greatest factor that inhibits performance is human doubt (and also noted how it is somewhat odd that few, if any, psychological papers have been written on doubt). In a group situation, doubt is contagious, and as it grips, it deepens—ultimately into panic. In a team, 'interference' is multiplied—no, squared—and, in the worst cases, performance diminishes to the point where one person could do the work of the team in a fraction of the time.

Some years ago, I began work with a team that was in disarray. The team had a set of very challenging goals to achieve, and a two-day workshop had been arranged to resolve a number of critical issues. The team had travelled to a good country-house hotel in the wilds of Wales and had arrived the evening before the workshop. No excuse to be late, then. At the agreed start time, half past eight, five of the eight team members were in the room. With mounting frustration, they waited for the remaining team members. By a quarter to nine, all the team members had assembled. There followed a heated argument about whether an agreed time meant the actual hour of the clock or, as three people argued, included a 15-minute margin.

In my role as coach, I could have closed down the conversation and pursued the agenda, but instead I watched as the conversation went on and on. After 45 minutes, I could bear no more. Here was a group of highly intelligent individuals—and a lot of interference. In this particular case, the conversation about 'time' was a surrogate for a deeper issue within the team. I got to the issue—the interference—by pointing out the amount of time they had spent on a relatively unimportant issue—a symptom—and asking what they thought it was symptomatic of.

At first there was no meaningful response, so I imposed a minute's silence. It was a long minute. At the end of the minute, one team member suggested that just perhaps within the team there were divergent opinions about a particular and important element of the vision: whether the business would pursue an internet strategy or a telephone-based direct-sales strategy. The team had fractured and aligned in two separate groups: one behind the IT director, who was failing and losing some credibility, and another behind a new arrival, an old-school retailer. We now had a pretty clear agenda for the rest of the workshop.

In the very same way that interference is either squared or multiplied, so too is the potential. Let me give an example. One of the places where the impact of being a great team, without interference, is immediately noticeable is in sport. When playing competitive tennis at a junior level in Ireland, I joined up with another boy, Billy, whom I knew only slightly, to play doubles. He was from the north side of the city of Dublin, and I was from the south side. Dublin is a small city, but the north–south divide is miles wide. I had not chosen to play with Billy, nor he with me. The Tennis Association decreed the pairing for the sake of the inter-provincial team.

Billy and I played quite well together, and even won a few tournaments, but there was something missing. And then, one day, something different happened. I can still remember the exact moment, just as I remember the court and the people who we were playing. In the middle of a rally, without a signal or a spoken word, I knew what Billy was going to do next and where he was going to move. I noticed my body moving into open space to cover a shot without any conscious thought. The play became relaxed and spontaneous, the two of us moving, changing positions in a perfect and harmonious dance. When one made a mistake there was no sense of blame or even frustration from the other, and there was as much joy in seeing your partner hit an awesome stroke as in doing it yourself. Not only did we individually give our very best performances but we also created something unique together—a creativity in the tactics of each point that left our opponents thoroughly confused.

This is an example of being a team without interference. I know that it only involved two people, but many people report similar experiences from other activities involving greater numbers of people.

So, what was it about our team that suddenly gave us greater performance? The inner game model that I described earlier—potential minus interference equals performance—suggests that since our team was not playing to its potential, the first thing to do would be to identify the interference. Back then, neither Billy nor I had the understanding to enable us to do that, but I will suggest a little later how we came through. It's easy, of course, with hindsight. All these years later I can identify a number of aspects of interference that may well have been getting in Billy's way, or mine—a desire to be playing with my usual partner, for instance, or frustration at being forced to work with someone I had not chosen; fear of being judged, fear of letting the other down, not understanding how the other thought. And many more, I am sure.

In that rally, however, we found relaxed concentration, a mental state in which we could perform to the best of our ability. What was different about this is that it was a shared mental state that resulted in more than either of us could have imagined. A kind of two squared, giving four. We overcame these interferences in an entirely unconscious manner. We had begun to trust each other while playing together over the summer months, and as we reached the final stages of the season, our goals became more obvious and explicit. Both of these factors, as I will show later in this chapter, can be developed through team coaching.

Let me give you another example of a team that succeeded in minimizing interference, to achieve flow. A colleague and I worked with a team that launched, from nothing, an innovative retail bank in the UK that became quite successful. The team leader, now the CEO of the bank, was and is a highly intelligent and intuitive man. He realized that to launch the bank on time and on budget, the team would have to come together in a unique way, whereby each individual's talents were exploited and the whole was much greater than the sum of the parts.

The CEO charged us with creating an environment in which they 'could have the difficult conversations quickly'. I remember one particular meeting where the team resolved an issue of great strategic importance in 50 minutes that the board of the parent company had wrestled with the day before, for three hours, without coming to a solution. The team had learnt to respect each other—to listen and to put aside personal agendas for the sake of the team agenda. On a really good day, they did not need our coaching or facilitation; their sensitivity to each other was such that they knew instinctively who had something of value to add, and if that person was interrupted or had not been clear in what they said, another member of the team would ask them to finish or ask a question to clarify the issue. It would be untrue to suggest that this team was always in flow—in team self two—but they became very quick at recognizing when they were not, and at doing whatever it took to get back into that mental state.

The purpose of creating and maintaining a team is to achieve higher performance. For a team to experience more of its potential, the interference must be reduced. Interference in a team might include the following:

- Lack of trust in other team members
- Fear of ridicule
- Fear of being dominated
- Pursuit of personal agendas
- Need to lead
- Lack of clarity about the task or the goals
- Pursuit of incongruent goals
- Hidden agendas
- Not understanding (or distrusting) each other's intentions
- No agreed process for working together
- An absence of agreed ground rules
- Rivalries
- No listening
- No meaningful collective work
- Beliefs and positions ('this is how things are or should be').

A team that is successful in reducing the interference will be characterized by the following:

- An apparent absence of hierarchy in relationships
- Listening and a desire to understand each other
- Robust, challenging conversations
- Clear feedback sought and given
- The pursuit of 'impossible' goals
- Focused activity
- An intuitive sense of where each member is and how he is doing
- Request and offers of help or support
- Flexibility in the roles and a willingness to cover for each other
- Creativity, imagination, and intuition as part of the toolkit
- Team members caring for each other and each other's well-being
- Fun, joy, and the simple pleasure of being together
- Silence and thoughtfulness before decisions and action
- Mutual accountability for the achievement of goals.

You may have noticed the correlation between the interference factors—and those characterizing their absence—and the conditions of flow as described in chapter 5.

If we consider team coaching from this perspective, the role of the team coach is, in part, to help the team to reduce the interference and to achieve a team mental state, or 'team think', as I call it. The rest of this section of the book is devoted to that.

The big three

There are three top-of-the-list, most-wanted elements to successful teamwork. If these are not present, the most massive interference is unleashed. To state them baldly here is almost prosaic, bordering on the self-evident, but my experience is that these three elements are almost always assumed to be obvious and clear to all concerned. The 'blindingly obvious' simply blinds, however, and failure is imminent. These three elements are **who, what**, and **how.**

When a group of people comes together to perform a task, each individual needs to understand **who** each person in the team is, **what** the task is, and **how** he or she is going to achieve it. The degree to which these things are not clear is the degree to which effectiveness is diminished.

In this context, to understand 'who each person is' means to have sufficient insight into them such that they can be trusted and their intentions are clear. The 'what' means that there is clarity about the task facing the group: why are they doing it, and what would success look like?

Interestingly, 'task' occurs at two levels. Level one is the final output—the result, the goal. Level two is often more difficult to discern because it is concerned with what needs to be done immediately next in order to move efficiently toward the level-one goal. The team may need to address a relationship issue in the group before they can discuss what might be a more obvious issue, such as a matter of strategy. If the team fails to address the level-two issue, they will certainly come unstuck when they discuss the strategy. The interference will block their capacity to have a meaningful, creative conversation—or, worse still, some people, whose buy-in may be critical, may simply 'sit on the side-lines' and at a later date claim they were never in agreement.

The 'how' is about the process of achieving the level-one aims. It concerns a wide spectrum of activities, from strategy and priorities to communication, meeting frequency, agendas, and ground rules.

The degree to which these elements need to be clear, understood, and agreed upon is dictated by the difficulty of the task. A group meeting to decide the allocation of car-parking spaces does not need the same level of insight and clarity into who, what, and how than one about a team responsible for the rapid construction of a $300m factory.

Reducing interference in teams

The ideas expressed below are intended to give a line manager or coach a sense of how to reduce interference in teams. This list is neither comprehensive nor exhaustive, and the exercises within can be made more sophisticated. Here I just want you to get the idea.

Creating a common vision *(what)*

Creating a common vision or set of goals can help to reduce interference in as much as it is tangible evidence that all the players are on the same side. The creation of the vision may also flush out disagreements about the direction the team is taking. A discussion early on in the life of the team that sorts out such differences reduces internal bickering and upset.

Creating a common vision can be approached in hundreds of ways. The simplest is to get each individual to write down his or her vision or goals and then read them out to the team. Other members of the team listen, and when the readings are complete, the coach asks the team to identify the common points and themes. The advantage of starting with the personal vision is that the disclosure begins to generate understanding, and therefore relationships, within the team.

Agreeing a modus operandi *(how)*

Once the vision and goals have been agreed, the team then needs to dis-

cuss how they will achieve them. The potential for friction within the team can be greatly reduced by creating an agreement about how the individuals will cooperate. The question for the coach to ask here is: 'What are the ground rules that would support this team in achieving its goals?'
Start capturing the suggestions on a flipchart without engaging in debate or assessment. When the team has run out of suggestions, have them select those ground rules that they are all committed to. These should be reviewed at subsequent meetings and can obviously be changed, added to, or removed. Ground rules might include agreements about the function and frequency of team meetings, the values that they will adhere to (honesty, respect, and so on), and when the team will decide by unanimity, consensus, or team leader's decision.

Disclosure of life and career goals *(who)*

This is a very simple team exercise, and can even be done over a meal or a drink. Give the individuals some time to prepare and think through their goals—to do it properly, the coach might work with the individuals prior to the meeting. The individuals then talk to the team about their personal goals. This exercise works because it builds understanding, and therefore trust.

Facilitating feedback *(who, but can drag up issues of what and how)*

I have already spoken about feedback in chapter 5. Again, this exercise should build understanding and trust in the group. The simplest method is for each team member to take a turn in the 'hot chair'. The other members of the team then give individual feedback.

Giving a standard format to the feedback can make this easier. For example:

> One thing I would like you to stop doing is …
> One thing I would like you to start doing is …
> One thing I would like you to continue doing is … .

Identification of internal and external obstacles (who, what, and how)

This exercise is a way of getting the team to identify the interference for itself. There is more ownership this way. The question to ask the team is this: 'What are the obstacles, within the team or outside the team, to achieving your success/vision?' The coach will then note down all the obstacles on a flipchart and ask the team to rank them in order of their impact on the team. The GROW model can then be used by the coach to resolve the issues, thus reducing interference.

Surfacing conflict

There will almost always be a tendency to avoid conflict, in life and in teams. If this happens, the team is stuck, and no meaningful work can be done. The coach's role is to notice the conflict when it rears its head and to ensure that the team talk it through. Arranging for the parties in conflict to state clearly their position is the first step. Ensuring that the opposing party listens is the second.

An option here is to get each party to state the opposing party's position. As a coach, you also need to watch that the relationships survive intact—or, better still, deepen—following the conflict. Questioning each party about how they feel about each other is a good starting point.

When a team is in conflict and is not making progress, try declaring one minute's silence. This is a very challenging and powerful technique. The reflection that the individuals engage in during this minute is undistracted and seems to bring them face-to-face with their integrity. At the end of the silence, someone will usually take the risk and say what needs to be said, thus unblocking the team.

Achieving 'team think'

The story of my tennis partnership with Billy is a good example of 'team think': we got to a point where we knew what the other was going to do. A specific request from the client I mentioned earlier in the financial services—to have the difficult conversations quickly—was in effect a request to help him and his colleagues get to a similar point. His analogy was with a rugby team in which each player simply knew where his teammates were, and so could pass the ball without even looking. In fact there came a time in this team when I, as the coach, was almost redundant, because the team members were so aware of each other and took such care of each other that they were coaching themselves.

This state of 'team think' is achievable, but it requires some effort. Even making progress on the road to team think pays immediate and noticeable dividends, however. This next section should give you further insight into this notion.

The stages of development of teams

There is some really good news about coaching teams, and specifically about reducing interference: most people want to be in relationships with those around them. And they want the relationships to be meaningful. Of course, they may have to unlearn some things before they can have those relationships, but at least as a coach you should know that, in this sense at least, you are working with gravity and not against it.

There is something instinctive at work that guides people toward greater union. I do not particularly want to get spiritual about this, but I guess it is a higher expression of what we are as human beings. As a team develops, and the individuals gain greater understanding of each other, the team passes through four stages. There are two relatively well-known models that describe this process. The one best known in the workplace is this one:

Forming → Storming → Norming → Performing

A less well-known model is:

Pseudo community → Chaos → Emptiness → Community

Both of these models have a lot to offer, and are quite similar. The second model is from a book by M. Scott Peck called The Different Drum.

His book is about communities, not teams, but the process the team goes through is similar.

Stage one

When a team comes together for the first time, even if some of the members know each other, there is an unconscious game in play. The goal of the game is that everyone should get on and that there should be no disagreement. The members play the game by a set of rules that preserve this balance. In order to preserve the balance, people pretend. They pretend that they agree with each other; they tell half-truths and little lies. It is like being at a party with people you do not know. 'Isn't the garden lovely?' a guest says. It is awful, and you both know it, and you hear your voice say: 'Yes, they must work so hard on it.'

This is not the atmosphere of a high-performing team, but it is where all teams start. In the workplace, the ground rules are different, but the game is the same. Everyone knows that George is manipulating the meeting, but the only time it gets mentioned is in the pub. Very little that gets said in the pub ever changes anything—and not just because it is not often remembered! In order for a team to be productive, it must move out of this pretence and get to a place where the truth can be told, and where people can be all of who they are. But there are one or two steps on the way.

Stage two

Individual differences are not permitted in stage one, but as the team sets about its task differences will arise. As these surface the team moves into a phase where disagreement, conflict and confusion prevail. The tendency at this point is often to retreat into stage one—pretence. Another thing that happens at this point is that the team members fight it out, trying to ensure that one version of the truth dominates, and try to convert each other to their own point of view.

From this place, again, no useful work can be done. The coach's job is to ensure that the team faces up to the differences. As the coach, you need to be attentive to a typical response of teams in chaos. Otherwise, they will blame you for it: 'You should have been a stronger facilitator.'

Stage three

This stage is the most difficult for the team to tolerate. In order for the team to progress, the individual members have to be willing to give up on their version of the truth, or reality, or the right solution. They have to be willing to embrace another person's point of view—or even their right to have a point of view. The second model is a more useful guide here. Teams will try to escape from chaos by imposing an order on things: they will establish project teams or subcommittees to come back with a recommendation.

This is all very well as far as it goes, but the team is still left with unresolved differences that are now probably even more difficult to get on the agenda. The first model does not serve us well here, in that the danger of 'norming' is that it is simply another version of stage one—pretence. To move on, the coach works with the team so that they listen to each other, acknowledge their differences, and learn to look at issues from the perspective of another.

A powerful technique to use when there is a conflict is to get one party to summarize the other's position, and then have the second party do the same thing. This flushes out misunderstandings, but more importantly it forces each party to understand the other's point of view. Once a team has completed this 'emptiness' stage, it is as if all the interference evaporates, and the team can enter stage four.

Stage four

The experience of this final phase can be very profound for the team. The team is fully present, not knowing, and without a personal agenda or any attempt to win someone over. From here, something magical can happen and the team can focus on its task. It is a space of creativity, insight, and imagination, from which it is possible to see an issue as it really is. Decisions can be made clearly and easily, and a new vision can be created with the full alignment of the whole team. The atmosphere in the room will be quiet, with a bubbling of joy and excitement just below the surface.

One of the signs that the team is in this stage is a reluctance among the team members to leave the room when the meeting is over. This is parting as such sweet sorrow, and it should be indulged.

Once the team has achieved stage four, it will carry that spirit with it for quite some time, and it will infect others that the members touch. But the team will not stay in this space. Stage four will, after a while, become stage one again, and from there the whole process recommences. This is not bad news, however—quite the opposite. Each time the team passes through the stages, the relationships deepen and become more resilient and trusting. The team, with help from the coach, also learns how to go through the stages, gets quicker at it, and becomes more skilled in reaching 'team'.

There are at least two ways in which a coach can use this information. The first is to simply notice the progress through the stages and let the model guide your interventions, and not to panic when it gets sticky. Stage two is uncomfortable but essential.

The second way is to reveal the model to the team and to talk it through with them. This will give them some security in the chaos stage, and give them useful information about how to move forward. Sometimes, when I have spoken about the model and the team that I am working with gets stuck, someone will ask: 'Is this chaos?' The very knowledge that it is allows them to persevere.

The GROW model in team coaching

Imagine that you have just walked into a team coaching session. You are there as an observer. The team meeting has already started, but you haven't missed anything. This team is composed of the managers of the IT department in a retail bank, so IT is really important.

Let me tell you who's in the room: from the left we have Sally, then Tom, Peter, Jucintha, and Frank. Frank is running the project. The coach is also the line manager, although some report to him through Frank.

> COACH: Let me just check my understanding. As a result of our last meeting, you went out and collected feedback from your internal customers. There are many good points in the feedback, like the quality of your solutions. The main area for improvement is in the

quality of the service you provide. Is that correct so far?
PETER: Yes. Pretty much.
COACH: Tell me what the specific feedback is.
TOM: The two main areas are that while the quality of most of what we deliver is seen as excellent, we are almost always late in delivery—in one particular case by six months.
SALLY: Hold on. It's not that simple. The customer kept changing their mind.
PETER: Then you should have changed the delivery date …
COACH: It sounds like there might be something to discuss there, but let's not get into the detail yet. Tom, you said there were two areas …
TOM: Yes. The other area is that some of what we have delivered has not matched the customer's need. Now in one case, at least, they did not discover this until the software was installed. And this is not a quality issue—the software works, it just doesn't meet all the requirements.
COACH: Were there any other significant points raised in the feedback?
SALLY: I think that one thing people are asking for is more support in the handover of systems and, if possible, for a short time afterward.
PETER: You know we can't give that. We're short-staffed as it is.
SALLY: Well, it's what the customer wants.
COACH: Given all of that, what would be a useful goal for this session?
FRANK: I want to know what we are going to do about it.
COACH: Fine. So what would be a goal for the session?
JUCINTHA: Maybe we could create an action plan to improve customer services.
TOM: We'd have to have an idea about what improved customer services would look like. A vision, or some goals.
PETER: That's all very well, but it seems to me that we've got a problem already. I'd like to understand that first.
COACH: I have heard three goals: to create an action plan, to have a vision or some goals, and to understand the current problem. Is that right?
FRANK: We could do all of that, I think. At least it's worth a try.
SALLY: OK.
COACH: Is everyone on board for the three goals?

VOICES :Yes.
COACH: Peter, what about you?
PETER: I think it's a lot to tackle. We always take on too much.
COACH: Are you willing to give it a go?
PETER: OK, but I'd like to start with examining the current problem.
COACH: Thank you. We've got our goals. And Peter would like to start with the current problem. Is that the best place to start?
JUCINTHA: It's as good as any.
COACH: So what is the current problem?
PETER: The way I see it, certain people over-promise to the client. And that means that we end up not delivering what was expected, or being late. We have to manage the customer's expectations.
COACH: When you say certain people, who specifically do you mean?
PETER: Sally, mostly. And sometimes Frank. But other than me, they are the only two people who agree work. So that has a big impact on the team.
SALLY: We keep having this conversation. I say that you do everything you can to give the customer what he wants and exceed his expectations.
COACH: That sounds like a pretty fundamental disagreement. Before we get into it, are there any other aspects of this issue?
JUCINTHA: I think we are understaffed. We need at least one more person. A programmer.
FRANK: I believe that the budgeting process is getting in our way. We hold some of the budget, the development bit, and the customer holds the implementation part. It makes negotiation very difficult.
COACH: So we've got a disagreement about what we offer the customer, a question about staffing, and a budgeting issue. Which of these should we tackle first?
SALLY: I am tired of the battle with Peter. I'd like to get that out of the way.
COACH: Battle. That's a strong word.
SALLY: Well it's what it feels like. Every time we start up a project, Peter attacks me.
COACH: Have you told him that?
SALLY: I think so.

COACH: To be sure, why don't you tell him now?
SALLY: Peter, you are constantly attacking me over what you call 'over-promising' and I call 'delivering a great service'.
COACH: What is the effect of that on you?
SALLY: It's exhausting and very frustrating. And if I am truthful I can get quite upset.
PETER: I didn't realise. I'm sorry.
SALLY: OK.
COACH: I don't know if you guys need to do anything to restore good will.
SALLY: Maybe. Off-line. Later.
PETER: Yes. We can fix a time.
COACH: OK. And we are still left with the issue of what we offer the customer. I understand the over-promising part. What's the alternative?
PETER: You've got to manage the customer's expectations down. The budget is limited, there's only a certain amount of time, and very often the technology isn't available.
TOM: I understand that, but my heart is with Sally. The job would become really boring if we just delivered the minimum. I need the challenge. I enjoy problem solving and the opportunity to be creative.
SALLY: That's exactly what I think.
PETER: But if you do that we all end up exhausted and constantly overstretched. And then you create more work by having to return to the customer to fix some part that didn't get dealt with properly the first time. More work.
TOM: Do you understand that that seems boring to many of us?
PETER: No. Well, of course. But don't think that I'm just some kind of boring bean-counter. I get satisfaction from delivering something that works.
COACH: Frank, where are you in this?
FRANK: I can see both points of view. I've just been thinking that what's going to matter in six months time is what our customers think of us. Because when the new performance management system comes online, that is how our performance will be judged.
JUCINTHA: Can I say something? I don't think it matters whether

Peter or Sally is right. I think that the customer is more important. I'm sorry to say this, but I sometimes think that Sally is so interested by the technology that she forgets the customer, and that Peter is so concerned about well, how shall I say it, getting the balance between home and work right, that he'll deliver the least he can get away with.

PETER: Another way of saying that is that Sally and I are concentrating on fulfilling our own needs and not the customer's. Right?

JUCINTHA: Maybe. I don't want to upset anyone.

TOM: It's an interesting point. What would have to change?

SALLY: We'd all have to focus more on the customer.

COACH: And what would that look like?

FRANK: Giving them what they want, what they really need.

COACH: How would you go about doing that?

SALLY: Spend more time talking with them.

PETER: Better analysis of the problem or need.

TOM: Being prepared to say no.

COACH: Any other options?

JUCINTHA: Involving them more in the development of the software.

PETER: I wonder, maybe on bigger projects, if we could get people seconded to our own team?

SALLY: The advantage in that, for the customer, is that one of their own team becomes the expert, and they would be less reliant on us. And we would be certain to get a better understanding from the customer's perspective.

COACH: Any more thoughts? No? So which of these options do you want to take forward?

FRANK: All of them, I think. But can we just hold off making a plan at this point. I'd still like to do the vision and that may alter the plan.

TOM: Good idea.

COACH: Ready to move on?

The Model T in teams

The concept of 'following interest' in teams may be difficult to grasp, what with so many different and potentially divergent agendas. The Model T proves to be a magnificently powerful technique in this situation. The model says that you expand before you focus, and in this way you stay on the player's agenda. I will take a snippet from the conversation above to demonstrate this:

COACH: It sounds like there might be something to discuss there, but let's not get into the detail yet. Tom, you said there were two areas ... *(Expanding/clarifying)*
TOM: Yes. The other area is that some of what we have delivered has not matched the customer's need. Now in one case at least they did not discover this until the software was installed. And this is not a quality issue; the software works, it just doesn't meet all the requirements.
COACH: Were there any other significant points raised in the feedback? *(Expanding again)*

And then, a little later:

COACH: I have heard three goals: to create an action plan, to have a vision or some goals, and to understand the current problem. Is that right?
FRANK: We could do all of that, I think. At least it's worth a try.
SALLY: OK.
COACH: Is everyone on board for the three goals?
VOICES: Yes.
COACH: Peter, what about you?
PETER: I think it's a lot to tackle. We always take on too much.
COACH: Are you willing to give it a go?
PETER: OK, but I'd like to start with examining the current problem.
COACH: Thank you. We've got our goals. And Peter, would like to start with the current problem. Is that the best place to start? (Focusing)
JUCINTHA: It's as good as any.
COACH: So what is the current problem?

Coaching teams—indeed, the whole issue of teamwork—is so huge that this chapter can only serve as an introduction. I hope, however, that it has been more than an introduction, and that you feel that you could make a start—and a difference—by coaching either the team that you lead or one that you are coach to, such as a project team that you are looking after. The key is to get started. You can only learn to coach by coaching.

COACHING AND GENIUS

– CHAPTER 15 –

Enabling genius

Coaching can be appropriate for topics ranging from the smallest things in life to the biggest, from the prosaic to the profound; from planning a simple task to gaining a better understanding of your life's purpose (if you think you have one). As you becomes more of an expert as a coach, you are better equipped to deal with the bigger issues, and can step away from what has been called the non-directive approach to a place where guidance, provocation, and challenge may be required—and can very effective.

I increasingly choose to work with people who are confronted with big problems or opportunities where they are called on to give something extraordinary—and I call that process 'meeting the challenge'. What I began to realize is that I needed a way of thinking—a model—to help me structure the coaching programme more effectively. This need was one source of 'enabling genius'. The second was noticing the abundance of literature on topics that relate to human potential, but not being able to find in that material a simple, comprehensive model.

In April 2013, I convened an international group under the banner of The Enabling Genius Research Project. The purpose of the project was (and still is) to bring together and make available the best research on developing human potential. This chapter provides an overview of that material, which, I hope, will be useful to anyone interested in excellence.

A brief story about genius

Only a few people get to be called 'genius', and most of them are dead. The rest of us—those that are currently alive—don't, and yet we have pretty much the same equipment as those that do. That's got to be interesting.

In the past, we have explained it away by describing the uniquely talented as 'having a gift'—from God, perhaps—or that it is 'in the genes', handed down from parent to offspring. Or, as you will hear if you watch sports on TV, that he or she is 'a natural'. I frequently wonder: who gets to set the bar above which one is deemed genius?

A really interesting thing happens when I speak about enabling genius. There's an initial fascination and curiosity. Then, when it becomes clear that what I am saying is that genius is available to all, and not just the very few, a good half of any group lose interest or become a bit defensive. To some, this notion of genius being available to all is a scary proposition—it is a challenge to their mediocrity, to their 'stuckness', to the notion that 'I am what I am'. Others seem to like the idea that genius is only for the few because they secretly think they belong to that set or have some power in the conferring of genius status. It's an elitist notion, and some people feel they belong with the elite (whoever they might be).

More alarmingly, a senior corporate figure responsible for the wellbeing and productivity of many thousands of employees (well, partially responsible!) recently told me: 'We don't want geniuses in this organization, we want people who will just get on with their job.'

So there is a sort of convenience in the conventional notion of genius. If genius is the preserve of the few, an individual can get on with being ordinary—which, to be fair, is what most people's education (religious and academic) has as its goal: ordinariness, mediocrity. And if I am one of those people in a position of authority maintaining that point of view protects my little world, my power.

Recently, an interesting piece of research emerged that challenged this conventional notion, and was repeated and apparently verified many, many times: the ten-year rule. The underlying idea is that people who achieved excellence, or world-class status, in their profession had practised for ten 10,000 over ten years. Some of the early research took place with chess players and then with musicians, but the findings hold true for the practitioner of any complex task.

Now practice, of course, is available if not to all of us then to a whole lot more than a few! There is the oft-told story of the father Laszlo Polgar, a Hungarian, who undertook to train his daughters to become masters in chess, and succeeded. Well, the daughters did—two, Judit and Susan, became grandmasters, and the third, Sofia, an international master. This compelling story is frequently used as an example of the rule.

Mozart is often upheld as an example of genius, and as a prodigy—that is, one who demonstrates virtuosity from early childhood, indicating that he is gifted, for he could not have been trained at such a young age. He was reputedly playing the piano by the age of three, composed his first music at five, and was taken on a tour of Europe at age six.

However, a closer look at his story is really quite revealing. First of all, his older sister was an accomplished musician who was taught by their father. From his earliest days, Mozart was hearing music and watching people play and practise, and after that—you might say inevitably—he started copying his sister's piano playing. Add to this that his father was a noted musician, composer, and teacher. His teaching approach was very progressive, and brings to mind the Suzuki method. His father set about teaching his son the minute he saw the interest and devoted a large part of his life to his son's talent.

Given all that input, it would be surprising if Mozart had been anything less than a genius. Here's another thing: there are those who say that Mozart's early works of composition are really not that good, and that it is only when he reached seventeen that he produced great works. That's about ten years—the rule seems to hold good.

What the ten-year seemed to offer, was a new dawn for the more liberally minded people involved in various professions, from psychology to education. But the story is not quite that simple. The first cloud to cross this early morning sun was the revelation that the ten-year rule was not quite so definite—in some cases, the number of hours was more like 4,000 hours, and in others 22,000 hours. The rule begins to look less like a rule.

Then it was observed that if you put someone who has demonstrated and early ability in a discipline alongside someone who has not, and then subject both to the same training, the one with the early ability progresses far more quickly than the other. Not *just* practice then.

Here's a great example. Stefan Holm, a Finish athlete and exponent of the high jump, put the hard yards in, did the practice, and perfected his technique over many years. Given that Stefan was somewhat stockier than the body type considered ideal for his chosen discipline, he is a great example of the ten-year rule. Indeed, he won the 2004 Olympic gold medal.

Then came the college basketball player Donald Thomas. In 2006, he was challenged by some of the athletic fraternity at Lindenwood University to try the high jump. He strolled up—in all the wrong gear, with nothing that could be called a technique—and cleared the bar. Within a year, Thomas was on the US athletics team, and at the 2007 World Championships he beat Stefan Holm into second place—after less than eight months of 'proper' training. Donald Thomas was born with abnormally long Achilles tendons, which act like springs, to propel him upward.
So, here's the thing—both athletes in their time were the best in the world. They just got there by different means. They had different kinds of genius. They are both genius.

You may be reading this and thinking that this is the old nature vs. nurture debate, and there are clearly overtones of that. 'Vs.' says one or the other, not both. In his book *The Genius In All Of Us*, David Shenk talks about interaction—the interaction between genes and environment. In the 'vs.' paradigm, the genes come first and dictate what one would become; in the 'interaction' paradigm, genes and environment interact to create a unique individual.

'Individual difference in talent and intelligence are not pre-determined by genes,' he writes; 'they develop over time. Genetic differences do play an important role, but genes do not determine complex traits on their own. Rather, genes and the environment interact with each other in a dynamic process that we can never fully control but that we can strongly influence.'

That we can strongly influence. What seems clear is that we are, in almost every respect—brain, mind, and body—far more malleable than has previously been thought to be the case.

Three Kinds of genius (+ 1)

The enabling genius proposition is that genius is an intent and a way of engaging that I can awaken in myself and inspire in others—to allow this instrument (me or you), with all its capabilities and limitations, to be expressed in a given moment.

It may be a particularly Irish use of English (since that is where I hail from), but I think many will have heard or used the phrase, 'That is pure genius!' We are most often not referring to the acts or products of a conventionally defined genius: they are referring to something that is perfect for its situation, complete of itself, and that is the act or product of an 'ordinary' person. A story told, a witty response, an advert on television, a sketch that captures the essence of its subject, a meal cooked with care and attention. We know it when we see it—' pure genius'.

Often, in the doing of the act or the making of the product, the actor or maker is completely focused, without interference, in flow. Being genius is about setting yourself up to have more of those moments, in more and different activities, more often. This is what I mean when I refer above to 'intent' and 'a way of engaging'.

There are three specific kinds of genius—and a fourth that is not the subject of the research project at the moment. There are:

Unique individual genius in a specific discipline, craft or skill set. This will often be how a person might define him or herself: musician, tennis player, architect. Within each discipline, these individuals will have their own unique way of going about it, like the high jumpers I mentioned earlier. I believe it is possible to be more than one unique individual genius at the same time. In fact, I think it may be a real help, as the learning from one discipline can show light on the other. And of course at different stages in life we may be called to develop different unique individual geniuses.

Genius in any discipline, craft or skill set. This suggest that an individual can engage in any discipline and 'be the best they can be'. I am not a particularly great musician, although many of my siblings are quite skilled in various musical disciplines. When I went away to boarding school, I was upset not to be included in the choir after an initial test. It took me a few months to summon up the courage to ask for a retest, which I passed, allowing me to join my friends in the choir. A few years later, I sang solo at mass in the school church in front of the entire school and the local community. Was I great? No, but I was the best I could be at that time, and no one complained.

Moments of genius. These frequently occur as spontaneous, unplanned events—some of the 'pure genius' events fall into this category. You are walking down the street and an insight occurs. Genius. A friend of mine was looking for a parking space and spotted a person getting into a car. He positioned himself to take the parking spot. Another car drew up alongside with an irate driver saying the driver of the parked car had promised him the spot. My friend instantly responded with a warm smile and said: 'Let's toss a coin for it.' The situation was instantly defused. Genius. Unplanned and unrehearsed. (And he won the toss.)

The forth kind of genius we identified is **collective genius**. This is where a group of individuals come together in a collective self two and deliver something extraordinary. It is not a topic for here—it's too big—but I need to leave a place-marker for it.

'It's like this,' a friend of mine observed. 'Any time you're walking down the street, wherever you are going, whatever you are doing, your genius is by your side. The only questions is—are you open to it?'

The pillars of enabling genius

Pillars, in the architectural sense, are the components that support a building. But they are not the whole building. The pillars of enabling genius do not collectively represent a model for the whole of genius and how one enables it. I suspect that domain is too great to be captured in any one model. The pillars are the principal ideas. Many of the things shown in one circle could appear in another, or in the overlap. For instance, I have shown 'values' in the 'identity' circle, but a value such as self-sufficiency might well show up in 'learning' or even 'mindset'. The proposition here is that the stronger each of the pillars is, the more likely one is to be genius. There is not space in this book to go through every aspect of the model in full detail, so the intention here is to give a strong sense of what it entails.

The Pillars of Enabling Genius

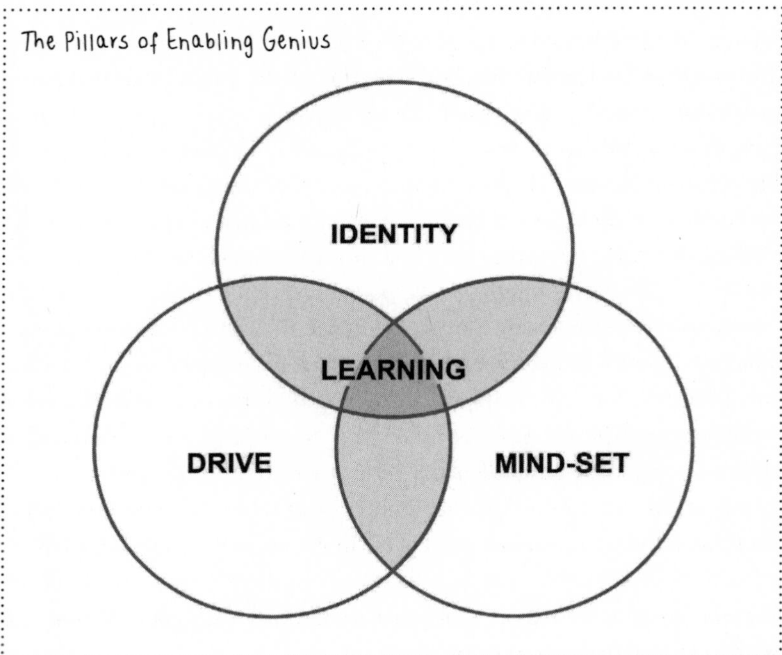

Learning

Why is learning so little loved? We so often approach it with an attitude of drudgery. Then there are those who think that they have demonstrated their success and have no need to learn. And yet learning is at the heart of genius—genius does not come about without it. For this reason, it is at the centre of the model.

I have committed myself to a 'genius project'—to get back to playing competitive tennis. Somewhat to my surprise, the greatest joy of my project is the learning. All the greats in whatever discipline have spent hours and hours practising and learning. A new challenge is greeted with pleasure, and to overcome it one must learn, change, adapt.

Roger Federer has been an extraordinary example in this regard. He lost in the semi-final of the 2011 US Open to Novak Djokovic—a match he was on the point of winning. His response? He went away, worked on certain aspects of his game, and came back with an extraordinary streak of wins. Then to 2013, which was a bad year for Federer as he struggled with injury. The pundits were writing him off. News leaked out that he had tried a new racket just before the US Open. In December, he worked hard with the new racket and added more power, more reach, and more spin, and duly retook his place among the top three or four players in the game. He then took on Stefan Edberg, a former champion, as his coach, and reached the 2014 Wimbledon final, narrowly losing in a classic match. Learning. Genius.

You may have come across a musician called Rodriguez who put out two albums that were not commercially successful. So he took on work with a small construction firm. Year later, when he and his music were rediscovered (seek out the inspiring movie Searching For Sugar Man), he stepped out on stage in South Africa as if he had never been away. But this is what's interesting: the owner of the construction firm had this to say about him: 'He keeps on refining the process of how he applies himself.' Learning. Genius.

Within learning I have also included three other categories. **Deliberate practice** is the term given to highly intentional, designed practice. One of the outcomes of deliberate practice is that the player moves complex, critical activities out of the zone of conscious thought and the activity becomes 'second nature'. This allows the skilled player, now that his mind is not preoccupied with the basics, to focus on higher order things. For a coach, this could be to observe the player's physical behaviour or how a proposed course of action might fit into a company's strategy, and to then use this this information in the coaching session.

The degree to which I am good at coaching is a function of the fact that I have had the opportunity to do an awful lot of deliberate practice—I have demonstrated coaching in public at conferences and workshops around that world many hundreds of times. This has meant that my coaching practice has always been the subject to scrutiny, questions, and feedback. There is a relationship here with unique individual genius: when I have clarity about my genius in a particular discipline, I can then identify the required deliberate practice.

Sport and many of the arts lend themselves to deliberate practice. It is more difficult in business, but finding ways to do so reaps great benefit. Aristotle Onassis, the Greek shipping magnate, is said to have practised meetings. Most of us complain about meetings, but what if you got really good at playing them? I have a coaching client who has mastered the fundamentals of meeting so that he can bring his attention to the others in the meeting, to likely consequences, to alternatives. The key to effective deliberate practice is to find the critical activities that support your unique genius, to get really clear about your intention in those activities and the desired outcomes, and then to find ways to practise them. That clarity of intention is also a great help in maintaining a self two mindset.

Reflection and ruthless self-appraisal—taking the time to reflect and appraise one's performance afterward—is another activity that leads to excellence. You will be hard-pushed to find a master of any discipline who is not self-critical. The aspect that is frequently missing is a certain ruthlessness—to be utterly honest with yourself. This is not an indulgence, and it must be done in such a way as to not feed self one by generating doubt.

Non-judgmental awareness is simple to say but not always simple to do. The point of taking the judgment out of the things you notice is that we tend to stay in self two—whereas judgment almost always puts us into self one. Think back to Gallwey's expression 'awareness is curative'. There is a great inner-game golf exercise to help people with their putting. The coach gets the player—often a novice—to hit a ball toward the hole and then to describe as accurately as possible where the ball stopped in relation to the hole, as in, 'Three feet to the left and one foot short.' The player is told to make *no conscious adjustments* but to hit another ball and describe the result.

To their surprise and delight, most players will put a ball in the hole after a few shots. In the world of business, this can simply mean rating a quality such as clarity, focus, or enjoyment on a scale of one to ten on a frequent basis throughout the day—and not making any conscious changes. Whatever the quality, it tends to become manifest in your behaviour. Enjoyment is a great quality to rate as, according to Gallwey and my own experience, it is the quickest way to self two.

Identity

This refers, most particularly, to the first kind of genius: unique individual genius in a specific discipline, craft, or skill. If I have real clarity about something, I can develop it. As I mentioned earlier, I have recently taken up tennis again. Given that the game, the equipment, and the techniques used have moved on since I played in my teens and twenties, I have taken on a coach, Craig, to help me learn. The tennis has become my personal 'genius project'.

Early on, Craig initiated a conversation about what defined me as a tennis player: how do I play the game? We spoke about some of the great players I saw as role models, and from this we began to create an image of my unique individual genius as a tennis player. This in turn allowed us to look at the aspects of my game that I needed to develop in order to play my best tennis—and, sometimes, to win.

As we were having the conversation, my mind was drawn back to a match I played when I was 17 that I could have won. What dawned on me was that, back then, I really had no idea about how to win other than in the most simplistic sense (hit it harder!). Without the clarity of my identity—my unique genius as a tennis player—winning was always going to be difficult.

Identity also includes one's sense of purpose, self-image, and the 'mental models' that one develops of oneself, the world, and what it takes to live in it. I have spent much time trying to build and run small businesses because I had it in my model (or 'personal construct') that you had to build a business to create capital value. That's all well and good, but I ended up doing things that I could (just about) do, and not doing what my genius desired. And that way lays a lot of pain.

Mindset

I have covered the idea of mindset in some depth in the chapter of the same name. I think there are two aspects to mindset that for want of better terms could be called 'surface' and 'deep'. Surface mindset refers to how I show up in the moment: am I focused, present, unworried, in self two? Or am in self one? Surface mindset is almost the filter through which one interacts with the world in a given moment. I can learn the skills of getting focused, present, and into self two.

Deep mindset, on the other hand, is more about attitudes and dispositions—fixed and growth mindsets, for instance. These don't just show up in the moment but persist over time. I can change or develop these attitudes and dispositions, but that takes time.

Drive

In an earlier version of this model, I had 'inspiration' as the title of this domain or pillar—there seemed to be something poetic about it, and it is unquestionably a key element. However, inspiration frequently comes from outside of the individual, and I don't like the idea of lots of budding geniuses sitting around waiting for inspiration to show up. So 'drive' seems a better fit. It describes more accurately the kind of energy and commitment one needs to bring to being genius.

Being stuck and getting **unstuck** is an essential component of genius. You have to inhabit your own authority—your ability to cause or produce—to be unstuck. Genius does not come from external motivation, but must come from within. Genius is self-expression.

I said above that **inspiration** mostly comes from within—the origin of the word is, after all, to breathe in. However, it is possible to find inspiration. It does require that you go looking for it. Once found, it is something you nurture, so that it becomes a source of energy.

We sometimes talk of **purpose** as if it, too, were an externally sourced thing—a direct link to a God or to Gaia. But purpose is something we make up for ourselves. Having a strong sense of purpose provides energy and focus, and is a component of your unique individual genius. It is worth working on.

Will is something you develop. Whether or not it is in the genes I cannot say, but I do know that you can increase it. A while back, I was recovering from injury and unable to go for my regular runs. The therapist suggested walking for at least an hour instead. On one occasion, I was becoming somewhat bored and thought of turning back early. The voice in my head—most often the voice of self one—piped up with a question: 'What does your will want?' My will, it seemed, wanted to continue walking. This was definitely a self two intervention, and a wonderful lesson: will is not a fixed quotient.

Enabling

A huge part of enabling genius is coaching, and the effective coaching model embraces many approaches, from following interest to teaching, that give the skilled coach a lot to play with. And yet I think that 'coach' and 'coaching' are not quite enough for the task. I prefer the idea of a guide. A guide is someone who knows the territory; someone who can steer the player away from danger and point him toward interesting and appropriate experiences, where the needed learning can occur.

I have a mental picture here of a kind of a golf course. It is different, in that there is no given sequence in which to play the holes. The player chooses where to go next. The holes are components of the pillars of enabling genius. The guide knows the territory, all the holes, and a variety of approaches to each.

The resistance

I cannot leave this chapter without talking about the resistance. Gallwey called it 'interference', while Steven Pressfield called it 'the resistance' in his book *Turning Pro*. Resistance is fear and doubt. It's self one. It's a fixed mindset. No one who sets out on the path to being genius is immune to resistance. Somewhere along that path it will rear up in front of you. The key is to see it for what it is: another fiction.

In a very real way, what I have just said is not fair. The brain is designed to be efficient. Change uses more energy than almost anything else, and so the brain will resist change: resist, but not totally block for all time. As a coach and guide, and as player, you need to be aware of this, and that the player is likely to feel like giving up on the challenge. Be gentle, and understand it as best you can—but don't stray from the path.

– CHAPTER 16 –

The art of coaching

I am coaching someone, a woman. We are in front of about 50 people at a conference. I have never met her before today, so I know nothing of her job, the company for which she works, the nature of the business, or her personal background. I am nervous, and a little distracted. I want to do a good job and present the effective coaching model as best I can. The subject matter of the coaching session is complex, and I am struggling to understand. I can hear in her voice that there is a little emotional energy wrapped up in the issue. I wonder if I would not have been better off if I had chosen someone else to coach.

I pull my chair a little closer and bring my attention back to what the woman is saying. After a few minutes, I stop her and give a summary of what I have understood so far. I can see she is a little surprised that I have understood so much, in particular some of the nuances. I ask if my summary is complete. No, she says, I have missed this bit, and then she's off again.

The people in the room recede into the background, and then they are gone. All my attention is with the woman and what she is saying. There is nothing else present in my mind. She relaxes a little more. I begin to notice little things: a hesitation, a slight grimace, an impatient gesture, a quickening in the pace of the talking, a change in the breathing pattern, a change of colour in the face. I notice my own response to what I am hearing and seeing, what I think and feel about what is being said. I notice a pattern in what I am hearing and seeing—faint at first, more of an intuition. Sometimes, I know what she is going to say before she says it. And then I begin to understand: not just the issue and its significance, but an understanding of this person, who she is and how she is playing out this part of her life.

I ask a question. It does not feel like me asking the question. I recognize my own voice—I can feel my jaw move, but the voice seems to be located about a foot behind my left ear and six inches to the side. In fact, a part of me seems to be located in the same place, because it is almost as if I can see from there, too.

The question—the culmination of all that I have learnt from this woman about the issue—is absorbed in silence. Then a smile creeps from the corners of her mouth toward the centre, and from there to the eyes. Something has been understood, reframed; a new possibility emerges. The coaching is over. The environment begins to intrude. There are some questions from the floor. No one has noticed what happened, save for me and, I think, my new friend.

When I am coaching—whether it is a demonstration in public or a conversation in a client's office—I occasionally rise above my normal proficiency to another level of skill and insight, where there is a greater fluency and not a little joy. In inner game terms, I am coaching from self two, a mental state that can be achieved when one performs with excellence, where all of one's faculties are available, and one's sensitivity heightened. This is pure flow.

The situation described above is typical. If my description sounds slightly 'magical', I do not see it as that, although we may have different definitions of the term. As a human being, that level of performance is available to me in any and every activity. In coaching, the player is communicating with much more than the words being spoken, and each coach is capable of picking up the messages and processing them. In fact, in every conversation we have, we are picking up these signals and including them in our responses—usually in a very unconscious manner. In self two, our observation is more acute; we pick up more of the messages and respond in an uninhibited and congruent manner.

This final chapter is about the inner aspects of coaching as I experience and understand it—not as a model to be applied to the player, but as a way of maximizing one's own performance. In the skills chart below I refer to the skill set involved in achieving this state of flow somewhat more prosaically as 'managing self', and I describe the intent as follows:

- to minimize the impact of the manager or coach's needs, preconceptions, judgments, and so on, on the player, and
- to maximise one's own performance while coaching.

As I have noted already, one of the core inner game ideas is that of 'potential minus interference equals performance'. There are two major interferences that I would like to address here:

- Trying to get it right
- The coach's possible thoughts, opinions, and judgments about the player.

I am reminded of a wonderful gentleman who, while learning to coach, came to a critical point in his own learning. He was trying very hard to get it right, to do it by the book, until he realized that this effort of trying was getting in the way of focusing his full attention on the player. In his next coaching session, he focussed more fully on the player, and his and the player's experience of coaching was transformed—it became a fluid and seamless conversation. His comment afterward was that the models and guidelines that we had been discussing up until that time were 'for the discipline of the novice'.

My purpose here is to make sure that, when coaching, you are not stuck in the purely non-directive—to free you from the potential tyranny of apparent 'rules'—so that it becomes possible to do what is appropriate in that minute for that particular player, and thus open the door to coaching as an art, as a form of self-expression. That coaching could be self-expression might occur as a contradiction, but to me the elegant deployment of all my skills is just that. It is for this reason that this chapter is called 'The art of coaching', and also why the definition of coaching given at the beginning of this book includes the word 'art'.

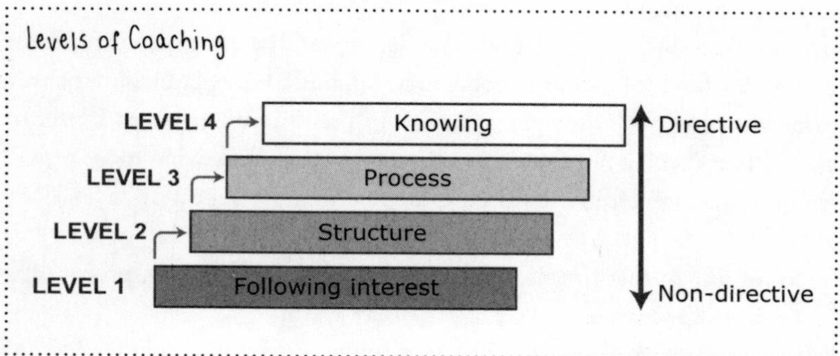

Trying to get it right

I need to make sure here that we do not get too precious about non-directive coaching. To do so introduces a significant interference. There is a very delicate balance to be struck here, because I do not want to give licence to those who might revert to type—or, more accurately, habit—and start instructing, making suggestions, giving advice or, worse still, attempting to control. The balance is between retaining what is vital in the non-directive model (ownership, responsibility, learning, high performance) and acknowledging that the person doing the coaching has intelligence, experience, intuition, and imagination—and that, in many cases, this will be of value to the player. Withholding a really good idea from the player would serve no one's interests, so I want to debunk the notion that there is a correct way to coach.

I remind you of the 'levels of coaching' diagram.

What I want to be really clear about here is that coaching from any of the levels shown in the diagram is valid as long as it passes four tests:

- It raises awareness in the player
- It leaves responsibility and choice with the player
- The relationship is strong enough
- My intent is clear.

One other thing happens as we move up through the hierarchy to the more directive approaches: it becomes more and more difficult to be effective. In fact, I would argue that you have to become competent at the lower levels before moving up. The irony is that, in traditional approaches, you start at the top—at level four. If you do not have some competence at level one, however, you are unlikely to know, when coaching from, say, level four (*knowing*), whether you have taken choice and responsibility away or have simply lost your audience. You are more likely to think: 'They just didn't get it. Are they stupid?'

My suggestion is that you build a strong foundation of non-directive skills, and that then with experience and experimenting you will be able to exploit the other levels—bearing the four tests in mind. It is also worth stating that I believe it is impossible—and perhaps not entirely desirable—for coaching to be completely non-directive. It is impossible because the slightest flicker of concern in the eye—the faintest smile of approval—will show up and be read and interpreted by the player. And so to the next major interference.

The mindset of the coach

The second major interference is the thoughts, opinions, and judgments that the person coaching might have about the player. A part of 'managing oneself' while coaching is to be able to identify one's own 'stuff' and to deal with it appropriately. 'Stuff' may take the form of notions and judgments that are not relevant to the player, but there will also be stuff that is relevant. Distinguishing one from the other is critical, but even more important is the fact that this stuff will almost certainly occur as interference for the coach, distracting him from paying full attention to the player.

One route to overcoming this interference is to have a frame of reference—a mindset—to bring to the coaching. I offer the following propositions as an appropriate mindset. I want you to know that what comes next is **not** the truth. It is merely a set of propositions. I find that by holding on to these propositions and operating using them as a basis, I eliminate much interference, and so I am a more effective coach.

I will give it to you straight first, and then explain it in more depth:

- People have huge potential
- People have a unique map of reality—not reality itself
- People have 'good' intentions …
- … and are achieving their own objectives, perfectly, at all times.

On first reading, people find this a bit difficult to swallow. Let me take it statement by statement.

People have huge potential

Most people have a belief or a point of view about human potential. At one end of the spectrum you have the 'you can't teach an old dog new tricks' brigade. They are joined by 'I am the way I am' and 'why should I bother?' These people do not have much faith in human potential. At the other end of the spectrum, you have 'I can do anything I can dream of'. When these guys are standing on a cliff, flapping their arms in a frenzied imitation of a seagull, this is cause for concern.

I do not know where you stand on the spectrum—I just know you stand somewhere. I suggest that neither end of the spectrum is particularly healthy. The question that we should embrace as coaches is this: Where on the spectrum should I stand as a coach, as someone committed to another's growth, development, and full expression as a human being?

In my story about Kevin, my assessment at the time was that the goal he had set himself was way beyond his reach. How wrong I was. To take the goal from him would have been to take away part of his life—a sort of well-intentioned murder. Daniel Goleman, in his book *Emotional Intelligence*, says that recent research suggests that we are only using 0.01% of our mental capacities as human beings.

What? I did the ball-catching demonstration described in the early part of this book at a small conference. The volunteer was a complete klutz. I noticed myself making this judgment in the first ten seconds—just in time to put it out of my mind. When the demonstration was over, the volunteer had surprised himself and the entire audience. I asked the group what they had noticed in the demonstration. The response that silenced the room was this: 'You believed in him, even when he didn't.'

People have a unique map of reality - not reality itself

You have a mental map of reality. Much of that map was created in the first few years of your life and has not been updated since. You operate to a large degree on the basis of this map. If you think of a journey you take regularly, you can probably visualize the route. You have a mental map of the route. A map—such as a road map—is a representation of the surface features of a territory in the same way that a menu in a restaurant is a representation of the food available. The menu is not the food. Eating the menu will upset your stomach—and the waiter. Equally the map is not the territory.

People, then, have a map of reality, but it is not reality. The way you think it is is not the way it is. The way it is does not particularly care what you think of it—it does not change for you. The fact that we have a map of reality—and not reality—might not matter if all our maps were the same. But this is not the case. Each person's map is different—a unique map of reality, not reality itself.

There are some people out there who think that the way they think is the way it is; when they say 'if I were you …', they are actually a little surprised that they are not. These people do not make good coaches.

People have 'good' intentions

'Good' is not a judgment that I, as a coach, am making. It is in fact an exhortation to a non-judgmental stance. While I may initially view something as in some sense 'bad', I should withhold the judgment and seek first to understand.

This suggests that most people—the very vast majority—have good intentions. They want to be happy and fulfilled, and for others to be happy and fulfilled. They want good relationships with people. They want justice for all, an end to starvation and hunger. They have good intentions in the big things in life and the small.

I think it is possible, too, that there is evil out there in the world, and that some people are evil. I think of some of the monsters of history who perpetrated the most evil deeds. But that is a matter for the psychiatrists. You may, of course, receive a request to coach someone with whom your values are in conflict, or be asked to work for an organization with which your values clash. And you may choose to walk away. But back to the propositions. This third proposition is linked to the fourth, which we discuss next.

People are achieving their own objectives, perfectly, at all times

This is much more difficult. The truth is, people get what they intend. The trouble is, they don't always know what they intended until they get it. This morning, a neighbour told me that overnight, someone had put a scratch mark along the side of his car. It was done with a sharp object, like a key, and means that the entire side of the car has to be re-sprayed. That represents quite a lot of money and a lot of hassle. My neighbour thinks that it was one of a group of youths who live at the other end of his road. On hearing the story, I was filled with righteous anger—'Kids these days!' But hold on: people have good intentions and are achieving their own objectives, perfectly, at all times. I cannot find the person who scratched the car, and even if I could, I suspect the answer to 'Why did you do that?' would be: 'I don't know.'

Maybe the youth was with his friends and scratched the car in order to gain acceptance in the group. Maybe he achieved his objective. That does not mean that there are no consequences, even unpleasant ones. And it does not mean that the action was justified within the majority of people's understanding of reality. But it does mean that in the youth's map of reality, the objective to gain acceptance had some priority.

Let me give you another example. I am thinking of the person who comes into work late and leaves early. He ignores the dress code and is surly to most of his colleagues, particularly those in management positions. His work is badly done and seldom on time. The temptation is to conclude that he is a feckless layabout. But that conclusion helps neither the manager nor the individual concerned. If a person has a position on a matter—that is to say, if he makes a judgment—then immediately and inevitably he creates the opposite of that position. This is the nature of opposition.

If the manager condemns the 'feckless layabout' as such, that person is likely to take the opposite position: 'Oh, no I am not'—a position they will defend with intelligence and determination. A pantomime follows: 'Oh yes you are!' 'Oh no I'm not!' In opposition there is no real dialogue. If the manager or coach approaches this 'layabout' on the basis of his judgments, they will not have a meaningful conversation about it, and nothing will change.

However, if the manager or coach engages on the basis that the individual has huge potential, has a unique map of reality, has 'good' intentions, and is, in fact, achieving his own objectives, perfectly, in that moment—then there is the chance for something to shift. Approach someone without judgment and with empathy, and something special occurs; he may let you into his map of reality and, in sharing it with you, may see it differently and may choose to alter the map.

I say 'may' because there is no guarantee. But empathy is a far stronger place from which to give feedback than condemnation. The apparently feckless layabout, for example, has an interesting recent history. He was offered a job in the department at a lower grade than before but was promised that the department's manager would be moving on in three months and that he was in line for the position. Then there was a reorganization, and the promise was forgotten. Now nobody knows what to do with him, and his problem is shuffled backward and forward between his manager and the HR department. If you had not been willing to listen, you would never have found out what lay behind his behaviour and attitude—you would have always regarded him as a feckless layabout.

A manager in an organization is sometimes faced with a difficult choice: whether to invest time in understanding a 'poor performer' or 'trouble-maker' (and it can be a lot of time) or whether to start disciplinary proceedings. The four propositions above do not say that people should be shielded from the consequences of their actions. People are responsible for the results they get in life.

Liberalism and authoritarianism—the traditional responses—both have the tendency to remove responsibility from the individual. Effective coaching is empathetic, but it does not hide from reality; rather, it raises awareness of it and leaves the responsibility with the player or the member of staff. Sometimes, the investment will just not be worth the potential return. That will be your call—but you might at least make that call bearing in mind my four propositions.

To reiterate, then, these four propositions are not the truth. What they represent is a mindset that may serve you in situations while you are coaching.

A garden gnome?

There is one final piece that I would like to leave you with to help you find your own 'art' in coaching—an insight into your particular inner game. Each of us brings something unique to anything we do, not least coaching, as the four propositions above indicate. Gaining an understanding of that uniqueness, your, genius as a coach, and of how it can help you considerably in becoming a more effective coach, and will add to the enjoyment of it.

Whatever your unique individual genius might be – your use of humour, your particular intelligence, or your type of professionalism—it will show up in your coaching. So it's best to understand what it is, and also to understand how it can influence your coaching, positively and negatively.

One of my colleagues, Judith, has a wonderful coaching exercise that can produce just such insights. It involves the use of imagery, as you will see. On one memorable occasion, she demonstrated the exercise, with me as the player, in front of a group of senior civil servants. It went something like this:

> JUDITH: Myles, if you would just relax and close your eyes. And I want you to identify an occasion when you were coaching. Have you got a situation?
> MYLES: Yes, I am with a guy I coach. I've been working with him on

and off for three years. We are in his office in the city, sitting down.
JUDITH: Anything else?
MYLES: Yes. I really like working with him. It's always rewarding.
JUDITH: OK. I want you to notice yourself sitting in the chair. Notice your feelings, the atmosphere in the room.
MYLES: Yes.
JUDITH: And now I want you to observe yourself as if you were at the door and could see yourself in the chair. What do you notice?
MYLES: I look comfortable, at ease, and also alert.
JUDITH: So you can see yourself in the chair. What I want you to do is to allow an image to come to you, an image for yourself, and allow it to replace you in the chair.

I have started laughing—no, giggling.

JUDITH: What's happening? (T*here is a faint giggle in her voice, too.*)
MYLES: I can't tell you.
JUDITH: Why not?
MYLES: Well, not in front of these people. They'll think I am mad.
JUDITH: Too late. Tell me what the image is.
MYLES: It's a garden gnome. One of those brightly painted plaster things.
JUDITH: What do you notice about it?
MYLES: It's bright yellow and red. A red hat. And, I think he has a fishing rod.

By now, most of the people in the room are laughing too.

JUDITH: A fishing rod?

She drew out more details and then moved the conversation on.

JUDITH: How do you understand this image, your little gnome with the fishing rod? (*No judgment there, then!*)
MYLES: This is the playful part of me. It is imaginative, creative, and fun. The fishing rod is about listening and understanding. I cast the

line a number of times on the water, asking questions and listening. There are a few nibbles and then a bite. This is when I really begin to understand—when we reach the heart of the matter.

JUDITH: And how does this serve you as a coach?

MYLES: It's about not taking myself too seriously, not trying, and staying in self two. It also makes for a more creative space for the person I am coaching.

JUDITH: And how does this part of you—the gnome—get in the way?

MYLES: That's not immediately obvious. It could be that I can sometimes upset serious people—and there are plenty of them—by appearing frivolous. I know this can happen. I think it's also that I can sometimes use the fishing rod a little 'directively'—that I seek for a meaning that might not be there.

The laughter had stopped at this point, because it was evident that I was learning in a direct and very powerful manner.

There is an epilogue of sorts. About a week after this demonstration, I was with a player who had a very stressful work life. He was in charge of a part of an organization of many thousands of people, working in an environment that was extremely political. The coaching conversation had become oppressive. I noticed that I was struggling to add any value—and, to tell the truth, I felt a little out of my depth (that old, familiar self one).

In the moment of noticing this I remembered the image: my garden gnome. I lightened up. I stopped the conversation. I declared that I was losing the plot. He said that he was too. The atmosphere changed. I summarized as best I could. I asked the simplest of questions: 'I understand that this is all complex, but how do you want it to be?'

I want you to know that this was not the 'right' question. It was a question formed by a garden gnome with the intent of freeing up a conversation. And it worked.

Postscript

Having an insight into one's inner game and having clarity about one's unique individual genius as a coach, balanced with the skills and models of the outer game is essential to effective coaching. Aldous Huxley understood this when he wrote: 'If you take lessons before you are well and truly coordinated you are merely learning another way of using yourself badly.'

APPENDIX 1

Counselling, mentoring and coaching

The purpose of this appendix is to attempt to satisfy the need to differentiate between some like skills. The manner in which I do so may not appeal to all, and may conflict with your own understanding. So be it.

I will start by trying to distinguish between counselling and coaching. After many years of trying, and many conversations, I have failed to come up with a complete and watertight distinction between coaching and counselling. The core skills involved in counselling and coaching—and indeed mentoring—are very similar, if not actually the same. These are principally the skills of listening and asking questions. They are the skills toward the non-directive end of the spectrum of coaching skills. For this reason, coaching and counselling are difficult to differentiate. But it is important to distinguish between the two, as a coach is seldom qualified to operate in the domain of a counsellor or therapist, and to do so is potentially dangerous.

The distinction that I play out below is appropriate for coaching that takes place in the workplace. Life-coaching, for example, may employ other distinctions. I make a distinction between coaching and counselling that works for me. I have got to hold up my hand here and acknowledge that many counsellors do not like this distinction, but for all that I feel it has a certain validity. Counselling is concerned with the individual, and with the relationship between the individual and the context in which he operates: his family and community. Since most counselling is remedial, the intent is to help the individual become 'whole' and to find his place with his family and community.

Coaching differs somewhat from this because it also takes into consideration the task or work that the individual is engaged in. Coaching is con-

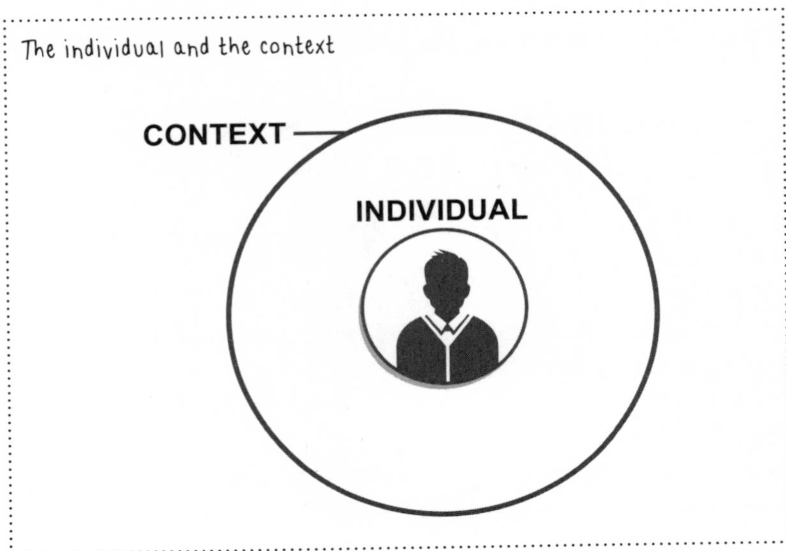

cerned with (a) the individual, (b) the relationship between the individual and his task or work, and (c) his context: the organization in which the individual works (see diagram below). The context also includes the individual's family and community, although these typically become a matter for discussion only if they are inhibiting performance of the task.

This gives us one guideline as to what the appropriate content for a coaching session might be. A topic gets on the coaching agenda if it relates to the successful execution of the task. So if the player wants to talk about the squash match they had with their best friend the night before, and how the best friend cheated, this is probably not an appropriate topic for a coaching session—at least not one on company time.

It is probably impossible to create a complete distinction between coaching and counselling. I know that as a coach I have had conversations, appropriately, with players that a counsellor could have handled just as well. What is important is not so much the distinction between the two but to know, as a coach, when you are out of your depth—when the skill and understanding that you possess are not sufficient to support the player.

The individual, the task and the context

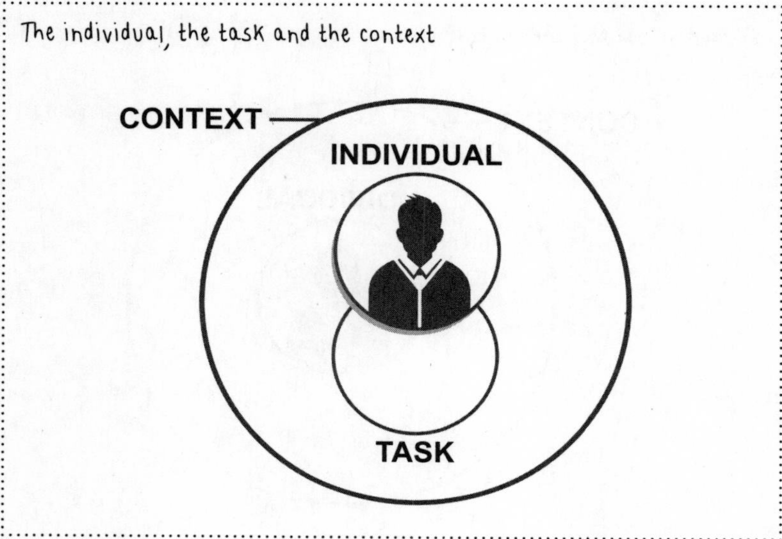

Fortunately there are some checks and balances:

- A player typically reveals only what he feels safe in revealing.
- Most players have an intuitive sense of what is appropriate, and of the skill and experience of the coach, and do not cross that boundary.
- The coach equally has an intuitive sense of what is appropriate and what he is capable of dealing with.
- A well set-up coaching programme will have a clear set of goals. If the coach is concerned that the topic for a session is not appropriate, it serves both parties to ask how discussing it relates to achieving the programme goals. This helps the player to stand back and reassess.

It is likely that at some point in your life as a coach you will find yourself out of your depth; that the conversation has a strong emotional content, and the player is in distress. The appropriate thing to do at this point is to stop coaching—to say explicitly that you want to end the coaching session, and that you want to end it because you are out of your depth.

Ask the player how he wants to take the matter forward and, if possible, guide him toward counselling or therapy. Be really clear that to stop coaching does not mean to stop listening. You need to stay with the player until he has regained sufficient composure to take the next step.

And, finally, to mentoring. A mentor is someone appointed or chosen to help another with the achievement of his or her long-term goals and career rather than immediate performance issues. The relationship is almost always outside any line-management relationship.

APPENDIX 2

Co-supervision exercise

The purpose of this co-supervision exercise is to ensure that the best interests of the player/subordinate and the organization are protected, and to provide educative and restorative support to the coach/manager.

This exercise should be conducted between two trained coaches. Experience suggests that the best way of doing it is to have one coach ask all the questions of the other, and for them then to switch roles. While it is possible to deviate from the questions, this should be kept to a minimum.

Contract

- Tell me how the stated purpose of the co-supervision exercise is relevant for you now.
- Tell me what you would like to achieve in this session (additionally, or more specifically).
- Tell me what your expectations are concerning confidentiality.
- Tell me anything else you need to say or do to be fully present.

Focus on the coach

- Tell me what I need to know in order to understand you, at this time.
- Tell me how that (the above) might impact your coaching.
- Tell me about anything else that you think might be relevant to this session.

Focus on the coaching practice

- Tell me what coaching you are engaged in at the moment (direct reports, others, formal, informal, individual, team?).
- Tell me any concerns you have about your coaching work.
- Tell me any concerns you have had over the past three months.

Focus on a case

- Tell me which coaching relationship/case would be most useful to focus on.
- Tell me what I need to know about that.
- Tell me about the contract you have with the player/subordinate (for example, goals or ground rules).
- Tell me what you find most difficult in this case.
- Tell me what you feel about the player/subordinate.
- Tell me what you think about the player/subordinate.
- Tell me what I need to know about the relationship between you and the player/subordinate.
- Tell me what your principal strategies are in working with this player/subordinate.
- Tell me how you are delivering value to the organization.

Focus on the coach - follow-up

- Tell me, as a result of this session, what you need to do for the player/subordinate.
- Tell me, as a result of this session, what you need to do for the organization.
- Tell me, as a result of this session, what you need to do for yourself.

Completion

- Tell me in what way I may have influenced this session.
- Tell me how I could have been a more effective co-supervisor.

REFERENCES AND FURTHER READING

The Inner Game of Tennis by W. Timothy Gallwey

The Inner Game of Work by W. Timothy Gallwey

Emotional Intelligence by Daniel Goleman

Focus by Daniel Goleman

Mindset by Carol Dweck

Flow and the Psychology of Happiness by Mihaly Csikszentmihalyi

A Brief History of Everything by Ken Wilber

A Different Drum by M. Scott Peck